OPTIONS STRATEGIES FOR TODAY'S TRADER

Featuring 50 Strategies for Bulls, Bears, Rookies,
All-Stars and Everyone In Between

RICHARD MAN

Table of Contents

Introduction

"An investment in knowledge pays the best interest."
- Benjamin Franklin

Benjamin Franklin's timeless wisdom resonates particularly strongly in the world of financial markets. Nowhere is this truer than in the realm of options trading, where knowledge truly is power. The options market, with its labyrinth of strategies and seemingly infinite possibilities, can appear daunting to newcomers and challenging even for seasoned traders. Yet, for those willing to invest the time and effort to understand its intricacies, options trading offers unparalleled opportunities for profit, risk management, and portfolio optimization. This book, "The Options Playbook," is designed to be your comprehensive guide through the fascinating and complex world of options. Whether you're a curious beginner taking your first steps into financial markets, an intermediate trader looking to expand your arsenal of strategies, or an experienced investor seeking to refine your approach, this playbook has something valuable to offer you.

Overview of the Options Market

Before we delve into the wealth of strategies this book presents, it's crucial to understand the landscape of the options market itself. Options are financial derivatives that give the holder the right, but not the obligation, to buy (in the case of a call option) or sell (in the case of a put option) an underlying asset at a predetermined price within a specific time frame. This simple definition belies the incredible versatility and power of options as financial instruments. The modern options market as we know it today has its roots in the early 1970s with the founding of the Chicago Board Options Exchange (CBOE). Since then, the market has grown exponentially, with options now available on a wide range of underlying assets including stocks, indices, commodities, currencies, and even other derivatives. The daily trading volume of options has skyrocketed from a few thousand contracts in the early days to millions of contracts today, representing billions of dollars in notional value.

What drives this immense popularity? The answer lies in the unique characteristics of options:

1) Leverage: Options allow traders to control a large amount of an underlying asset with a relatively small investment, amplifying potential returns (and risks).

2) Flexibility: With options, traders can profit from market movements in any direction - up, down, or sideways.

3) Risk Management: Options can be used to hedge existing positions, protecting portfolios from adverse market moves.

4) Defined Risk: For buyers of options, the maximum possible loss is known upfront and limited to the premium paid.

5) Income Generation: Strategies like covered calls allow investors to generate additional income from their existing stock holdings.

6) Speculation: Options provide a way to speculate on future price movements with limited capital at risk.

These features make options an invaluable tool in the modern investor's toolkit. However, with great power comes great responsibility. The leverage that makes options attractive also increases risk. The complexity that provides flexibility can lead to confusion and costly mistakes if not properly understood. This is where education becomes paramount.

Importance of Understanding Options Strategies

The options market is not a place for the unprepared. Unlike simpler investments like stocks or bonds, where an investor might reasonably expect to profit simply from the general upward trajectory of markets over time, options require a more active and informed approach. Here's why a deep understanding of options strategies is crucial:

1) Risk Management: Options can be powerful risk management tools, but only if used correctly. A misunderstood or misapplied options strategy can actually increase risk rather than mitigate it. Understanding how different strategies behave under various market conditions is essential for effective risk management.

2) Profit Maximization: The options market offers numerous ways to profit from a given market outlook. Knowing which strategy is most appropriate for a particular situation can significantly enhance returns.

3) Cost Efficiency: Many options strategies allow traders to express their market views more cost-effectively than simply buying or selling the underlying asset. However, identifying these opportunities requires a solid grasp of options mechanics and pricing.

4) Adaptability: Market conditions are constantly changing. A trader armed with a diverse repertoire of options strategies can adapt to these changes, finding opportunities where others see obstacles.

5) Avoiding Pitfalls: The options market has its share of traps for the unwary. Understanding common pitfalls and how to avoid them can save traders from costly mistakes.

6) Regulatory Compliance: Options trading is subject to various regulations designed to protect investors. Understanding these rules and how they apply to different strategies is essential for staying compliant.

7) Professional Growth: For those considering a career in finance, a strong foundation in options is increasingly valuable. Many roles in trading, risk management, and quantitative finance require options expertise.

The strategies presented in this book are not merely theoretical constructs. They are battle-tested techniques used by professional traders and institutions worldwide. By mastering these strategies, you'll be equipping yourself with the same tools used by the most sophisticated participants in the financial markets.

Brief Description of the Book's Structure and Objectives

"The Options Playbook" is designed to be both comprehensive and accessible. We've structured the book to cater to readers at all levels of options trading experience, from complete beginners to seasoned professionals. Here's what you can expect:

1) Foundational Knowledge: We begin with a thorough explanation of options basics, including terminology, mechanics, and fundamental concepts. This section ensures that all readers, regardless of their starting point, have a solid foundation to build upon.

2) Strategy Categorization: The 50 strategies featured in this book are carefully organized into categories based on market outlook (bullish, bearish, neutral), complexity level (basic, intermediate, advanced), and purpose (income generation, speculation, hedging). This structure allows readers to easily find strategies that match their market view and experience level.

3) In-Depth Strategy Explanations: Each strategy is explained in detail, covering:

- The market outlook it's designed for

- Its risk-reward profile

- Step-by-step instructions for implementation

- Potential adjustments and exit strategies

- Real-world examples and case studies

4) Visual Aids: Complex concepts are illustrated with clear diagrams, payoff graphs, and other visual aids to enhance understanding.

5) Risk Management: Throughout the book, we emphasize the importance of risk management. Each strategy discussion includes a thorough analysis of potential risks and how to mitigate them.

6) Practical Tips: Alongside the strategies, we provide practical tips and insights drawn from the experiences of successful options traders.

7) Market Context: To help readers understand when and why to use particular strategies, we provide discussions of market conditions and scenarios where each strategy might be most appropriate.

8) Advanced Topics: For more experienced readers, we delve into advanced topics such as volatility trading,

options on futures, and the use of options in portfolio management.

9) Regulatory and Tax Considerations: We provide an overview of key regulatory issues and tax implications related to options trading, with the caveat that readers should consult with legal and tax professionals for advice specific to their situation.

10) Resources for Continued Learning: The book concludes with a curated list of resources for further study, including recommended books, websites, and tools for options analysis.

The primary objectives of "The Options Playbook" are:

1) To demystify options trading, making it accessible to a wide audience.

2) To provide a comprehensive reference guide that traders can return to again and again as they progress in their options journey.

3) To equip readers with a diverse array of strategies, enabling them to navigate various market conditions.

4) To foster a deep understanding of risk management in options trading.

5) To inspire confidence in readers, empowering them to incorporate options into their investment approach.

Remember, while this book provides a wealth of information and strategies, it's important to approach options trading with caution and continued learning. Paper trading or using small positions to start is often advisable when implementing new strategies. Additionally, always consider your own risk tolerance and investment goals when choosing strategies to employ. As we embark on this exploration of the options market, keep Benjamin Franklin's words in mind. The knowledge you gain from this book is an investment – one that has the potential to pay substantial dividends in your trading career. So, let's turn the page and begin our journey into the world of options, where opportunity awaits those armed with knowledge and strategy.

Chapter One

Understanding the Basics of Options

What Are Options?

"The more you know, the more you realize you don't know."

- Aristotle

Options are financial instruments that derive their value from an underlying asset, such as stocks, indices, commodities, or currencies. At their core, options are contracts that give the holder the right, but not the obligation, to buy or sell the underlying asset at a specified price within a predetermined time frame. This fundamental characteristic is what sets options apart from other financial instruments and provides them with their unique flexibility and power. The world of options is primarily divided into two main types: calls and puts. A call option gives the holder the right to buy the underlying asset, while a put option provides the right to sell the underlying asset. This simple distinction forms the basis for all options strategies, from the most basic to the most complex. When you purchase a call option, you're essentially betting that the price of the underlying asset will rise. The call option gives you the right to buy the asset at a predetermined price (known as the strike price) before or at a specific date (the expiration date). If the market price of the underlying asset rises above the strike price, your call option becomes valuable. You can either exercise the option to buy the asset at the lower strike price and immediately sell it at the higher market price for a profit, or you can sell the option itself, which will have increased in value.

Conversely, a put option gives you the right to sell the underlying asset at the strike price before or at the expiration date. Put options increase in value when the price of the underlying asset falls below the strike price. If you own a put option and the asset's price drops, you could exercise your right to sell the asset at the higher strike price, even though its current market value is lower. Alternatively, you could sell the put option, which would have gained value as the asset's price declined. To navigate the options market effectively, it's crucial to familiarize yourself with the basic terminology. Key terms include the underlying asset, strike price, expiration date, premium, in-the-money (ITM), at-the-money (ATM), out-of-the-money (OTM), intrinsic value, time value, and the Greeks. Each of these terms plays a vital role in understanding how options work and how to trade them effectively.

The underlying asset is the financial instrument upon which the option is based. The strike price, also known as the exercise price, is the price at which the option holder can buy (for a call) or sell (for a put) the underlying asset. The expiration date is when the option contract becomes void, and the premium is the price of the option contract itself. An option is considered in-the-money when its exercise would result in a profit, at-the-money when the strike price is equal to or very close to the current price of the underlying asset, and out-of-the-money when its exercise would result in a loss. The intrinsic value is the amount by which an option is in-the-money, while the time value is the portion of the option's premium that exceeds its intrinsic value. The Greeks, which include Delta, Gamma, Theta, Vega, and Rho, are measures of an option's sensitivity to various factors. These will be explored in more detail in later chapters, as they play a crucial role in more advanced options strategies. Understanding the key players in the options market is also essential for grasping how options work. The main participants include option buyers (holders), option sellers (writers), market makers, brokers, clearing houses, and regulators. Each of these players has a specific role that contributes to the functioning of the options market.

Option buyers purchase options and have the right to exercise them, while option sellers receive the premium but are obligated to fulfill the contract if exercised. Market makers provide liquidity by continuously quoting bid and ask prices, and brokers execute trades on behalf of buyers and sellers. Clearing houses ensure the smooth functioning of the market by acting as intermediaries, and regulators oversee the market to ensure fair practices and protect investors. It's important to note that options can be traded on various underlying assets. While stock options are perhaps the most well-known, options are also available on indices, Exchange Traded Funds (ETFs), commodities, and currencies. Each type of underlying asset has its own characteristics that can affect option pricing and behavior. The flexibility of options allows for a wide range of strategies to be employed. Investors and traders use options for various purposes, including speculation, hedging, income generation, and leverage. Speculation involves betting on the direction of price movements in the underlying asset. Hedging using options to protect existing positions against adverse price movements. Income generation strategies, like covered call writing, can provide additional income from existing stock holdings. Leverage allows traders to control a large amount of the underlying asset with a relatively small investment. As we progress through this book, we'll explore these applications in detail, providing you with a comprehensive toolkit for navigating the options market. Remember, while options can offer significant advantages, they also come with risks. The leverage that makes options attractive can also lead to substantial losses if not managed properly. As we delve deeper into options strategies in the coming chapters, we'll always emphasize the importance of understanding and managing these risks.

How Options Work

Understanding the mechanics of options trading is crucial for anyone looking to navigate this complex financial landscape. At its core, options trading involves the buying and selling of contracts that grant the right, but not the obligation, to buy or sell an underlying asset at a predetermined price within a specific time frame. This simple concept opens up a world of possibilities for traders and investors, allowing for strategies that can profit from market movements in any direction, provide income, or protect existing positions.

The process of trading options begins with the creation of an options contract. This typically occurs when a trader, known as the option writer or seller, creates a new options contract and sells it to another trader, the option buyer or holder. The option writer receives a premium, which is the price of the option, in exchange for taking on the obligation to buy or sell the underlying asset if the option is exercised. The option buyer pays this premium for the right to exercise the option if they choose to do so. When trading options, it's important to understand that for every buyer, there must be a seller, and vice versa. This creates a zero-sum game, where one party's gain is another party's loss. However, unlike some other financial instruments, options allow both parties to potentially benefit depending on their goals and market movements. For example, an investor might sell a call option on a stock they own to generate income, while the buyer of that call option might be looking for leveraged exposure to potential upside in the stock. Options contracts are standardized, meaning they have specific terms that are consistent across all contracts for a particular underlying asset. These terms include the underlying asset, the contract size (how much of the underlying asset one contract represents), the strike price, and the expiration date. This standardization makes options more liquid and easier to trade, as all market participants are dealing with the same contract specifications.

One of the key elements in options trading is the concept of expiration dates. Every option contract has an expiration date, which is the last day on which the option can be exercised. After this date, the option ceases to exist and becomes worthless. Expiration dates can range from as short as one day to several years, depending on the type of option. Weekly options expire every Friday, monthly options typically expire on the third Friday of each month, and longer-term options, known as LEAPS (Long-term Equity AnticiPation Securities), can have expiration dates up to three years in the future. The choice of expiration date is crucial in options trading. Shorter-term options are generally less expensive but require the underlying asset to move quickly for the trade to be profitable. They're often used for short-term trading strategies or to hedge against specific events. Longer-term options are more expensive but give the underlying asset more time to move, making them suitable for longer-term strategies or for investors who want to gain exposure to an asset without immediately committing the full amount of capital required to purchase it outright. Alongside expiration dates, strike prices are another fundamental concept in options trading. The strike price, also known as the exercise price, is the price at which the option holder can buy (for a call) or sell (for a put) the underlying asset if they choose to exercise the option. Strike prices are set at standardized intervals, which can vary depending on the price of the underlying asset and the rules of the particular options exchange. The relationship between the current market price of the underlying asset and the strike price of an option is crucial in determining the option's value and behavior. This relationship gives rise to the concepts of in-the-money, at-the-money, and out-of-the-money options.

An option is considered in-the-money (ITM) when its exercise would result in a profit, not accounting for the premium paid. For a call option, this means the current market price of the underlying asset is above the strike price. For a put option, it means the current market price is below the strike price. In-the-money options have intrinsic value, which is the amount by which they are in-the-money. For example, if a stock is trading at $55 and you hold a call option with a strike price of $50, the option is $5 in-the-money and has an intrinsic value of $5. At-the-money (ATM) options are those where the strike price is equal to or very close to the current market price of the underlying asset. These options have no intrinsic value but may still have value due to the time remaining until expiration and the potential for the underlying asset to move in a favorable direction. Out-of-the-money (OTM) options are those where exercising the option would result in a loss, not accounting for the premium paid. For call options, this means the strike price is above the current market price, while for put options, the strike price is below the current market price. Out-of-the-money options have no intrinsic value and derive their entire value from the potential for the underlying asset to move in a favorable direction before expiration.

The moneyness of an option significantly affects its behavior and value. In-the-money options are more responsive to changes in the price of the underlying asset and are more expensive due to their intrinsic value. Out-of-the-money options are less expensive but require a larger move in the underlying asset to become profitable. At-the-money options are often considered to have the best balance of potential reward to cost, as they're less expensive than in-the-money options but more likely to become profitable than out-of-the-money options. When trading options, it's crucial to understand how these factors interact. For example, as an option gets closer to expiration, its time value decreases, a phenomenon known as time decay. This decay accelerates as expiration approaches, which can significantly impact the profitability of options trades. Time decay affects out-of-the-money options most severely, as they have no intrinsic value to fall back on. Another important aspect of options mechanics is the concept of exercise and assignment. When an option holder exercises their option, they're choosing to use their right to buy (for a call) or sell (for a put) the underlying asset at the strike price. This process is called exercise. On the other side of this transaction, the option writer who sold the option is obligated to fulfill the contract. This is called assignment.

American-style options can be exercised at any time up to and including the expiration date, while European-style options can only be exercised on the expiration date itself. Most stock options are American-style, while index options are typically European-style. It's important to note that most options are not exercised but are instead bought and sold on the open market before expiration. The decision to exercise an option depends on various factors, including the option's moneyness, the time remaining until expiration, and the trader's specific strategy and goals. In many cases, it's more advantageous to sell an in-the-money option rather than exercise it, as this allows the trader to capture both the intrinsic value and any remaining time value. Options also provide leverage, allowing traders to control a large amount of the underlying asset with a relatively small investment. This leverage can amplify both gains and losses, making options a powerful but potentially risky tool. For example, if a stock moves up by 5%, a call option on that stock might increase in value by 50% or more, depending on its strike price and time to expiration.

However, this leverage works both ways. If the stock moves in the unfavorable direction, the option can lose value much more quickly than the stock itself. In fact, options can expire worthless if they're out-of-the-money at expiration, resulting in a 100% loss of the premium paid. This potential for total loss of the investment is a key risk in options trading that all traders must be aware of and manage carefully. Understanding these mechanics is crucial for successful options trading. They form the foundation upon which all option strategies are built, from simple directional bets to complex multi-leg strategies designed to profit from specific market scenarios. As we progress through this book, we'll explore how these basic mechanics can be combined and leveraged to create a wide range of trading strategies suitable for various market conditions and trader objectives.

The Benefits of Trading Options

Options trading offers a multitude of benefits that attract investors and traders from various backgrounds and with different financial goals. These advantages range from enhanced leverage and cost efficiency to unparalleled flexibility and powerful risk management capabilities. Understanding these benefits is crucial for anyone considering incorporating options into their investment strategy. One of the most significant advantages of trading options is the leverage they provide. Leverage allows traders to control a large amount of an underlying asset with a relatively small investment. When you buy an option, you're essentially gaining exposure to the price movements of the underlying asset without having to purchase the asset outright. This leverage can lead to amplified returns if the trade moves in your favor. For example, if a stock is trading at $100, you might be able to buy a call option for $5 that gives you the right to purchase 100 shares at $105. If the stock price rises to $110, your option might be worth $10 or more, representing a 100% gain on your investment, while the stock itself only increased by 10%.

This leverage also contributes to the cost efficiency of options trading. Instead of tying up a large amount of capital to buy shares of a stock outright, you can gain exposure to the same number of shares for a fraction of the cost by purchasing options. This allows traders to potentially profit from price movements in expensive stocks or indices that might otherwise be out of reach. Additionally, the defined risk nature of buying options means you know your maximum potential loss upfront – it's limited to the premium you paid for the option. However, it's important to note that while leverage can amplify gains, it can also magnify losses. If the underlying asset moves against your position, you can lose your entire investment in the option. This is why proper risk management is crucial in options trading, and why it's often recommended that beginners start with simpler strategies and smaller position sizes as they learn the ropes. The flexibility offered by options trading is another major benefit that sets it apart from other forms of investing. Options allow traders to profit from a wide range of market scenarios – whether the market is going up, down, or sideways. This is in contrast to traditional stock investing, where profits typically only come from upward price movements (unless you're short selling, which comes with its own set of risks). With options, you can construct strategies to profit from specific price movements, time decay, or changes in volatility. For example, if you believe a stock will remain relatively stable, you might use a strategy like a short strangle or an iron condor to profit from time decay. If you expect a big move in either direction but aren't sure which way, you could use a long straddle strategy. This flexibility allows traders to fine-tune their approach based on their market outlook and risk tolerance.

Strategic advantages of options trading extend beyond just directional bets. Options can be used to generate income, hedge existing positions, or even take advantage of pricing inefficiencies in the market. For instance, the covered call strategy allows stock owners to generate additional income by selling call options against their holdings. This can enhance overall portfolio returns, especially in flat or slightly bullish markets. Options also provide unique opportunities for speculation with defined risk. Traders can take positions on specific events, earnings announcements, or anticipated market moves without risking more than the premium paid for the options. This allows for more precise and controlled speculation compared to outright stock purchases or short sales. Perhaps one of the most valuable benefits of options is their potential for risk management and hedging. Options can be used to protect existing positions against adverse price movements, essentially acting as a form of insurance for your portfolio. For example, if you own shares of a stock, you could buy put options to protect against potential downside. If the stock price falls, the increasing value of the put options would offset some or all of the losses in the stock position.

This hedging capability is particularly valuable for large institutional investors and portfolio managers who need to manage risk across diverse holdings. Options allow them to fine-tune their risk exposure without having to liquidate large positions, which could be costly and potentially impact market prices. Options can also be used to hedge against various types of risk beyond just price movements. For instance, options on volatility indices can be used to hedge against overall market volatility. Currency options can help multinational corporations manage foreign exchange risk. Even commodity options can be used by businesses to hedge against fluctuations in input costs. The risk management potential of options extends to individual investors as well. For example, if you're concerned about a potential market downturn but don't want to sell your long-term stock holdings, you could buy protective put options on a broad market index. This would provide a level of portfolio protection without the need to alter your core investment strategy.

It's worth noting that while options can be powerful risk management tools, they require careful implementation and ongoing management. Improper use of options for hedging can actually increase risk rather than mitigate it. This underscores the importance of education and potentially seeking professional advice when implementing complex options strategies. Another benefit of options trading is the potential for enhanced portfolio diversification. Options allow investors to gain exposure to a wide range of assets and market sectors without the need for significant capital outlay. This can help spread risk across different areas of the market and potentially smooth out overall portfolio returns. Options also offer unique opportunities for tax management. In some jurisdictions, options may be treated differently for tax purposes compared to outright stock ownership. This can potentially allow for more efficient tax planning, although it's always important to consult with a tax professional for advice tailored to your specific situation.

Lastly, the options market itself can provide valuable information for all market participants, even those who don't actively trade options. The pricing of options reflects the market's expectations about future price movements and volatility. Metrics derived from options pricing, such as implied volatility, can provide insights into market sentiment and potential future price action. While the benefits of options trading are numerous, it's crucial to approach options with a full understanding of their mechanics and risks. Options are complex instruments that require ongoing education and careful risk management. The leverage that makes options attractive can also lead to significant losses if not managed properly. Additionally, options have a time component, meaning they can expire worthless if your market view doesn't materialize within the option's lifespan.

The Risks of Trading Options

While options trading offers numerous benefits, it's equally important to understand and appreciate the risks involved. Options are complex financial instruments that can lead to significant losses if not used properly. A thorough understanding of these risks is essential for any trader looking to incorporate options into their investment strategy. One of the primary risks in options trading is the potential for substantial losses. When buying options, the maximum loss is limited to the premium paid for the option. However, this can still represent a 100% loss of your investment if the option expires worthless. For example, if you buy a call option for $500 and the underlying stock price doesn't rise above the strike price by expiration, your entire $500 investment is lost. This risk is particularly acute with out-of-the-money options, which require significant price movements in the underlying asset to become profitable.

The risk profile becomes even more complex when selling options. When you sell an option, you receive the premium upfront, but you take on potentially unlimited risk. For instance, if you sell a naked call option (selling a call without owning the underlying stock), your potential loss is theoretically unlimited if the stock price rises significantly. While such extreme scenarios are rare, they can and do happen, particularly during periods of high market volatility or in response to unexpected news events. Volatility is another crucial risk factor in options trading. Options prices are highly sensitive to changes in the implied volatility of the underlying asset. Implied volatility reflects the market's expectation of future price fluctuations. When implied volatility increases, option prices tend to rise, and when it decreases, option prices typically fall. This means that even if your directional view on the underlying asset is correct, you can still lose money if there's an unfavorable change in implied volatility. Volatility risk is particularly relevant for options sellers. Many popular income-generating strategies, such as selling covered calls or cash-secured puts, can perform poorly during periods of increased market volatility. Sudden spikes in volatility can cause the value of short option positions to rise dramatically, potentially leading to significant losses.

Time decay, also known as theta, is another critical risk factor in options trading. All else being equal, options lose value as they approach expiration. This time decay accelerates in the final weeks and days before expiration. For options buyers, time decay works against you, eroding the value of your options even if the price of the underlying asset doesn't move. For options sellers, time decay can work in your favor, but it also increases the risk of early assignment as expiration approaches. The impact of time decay is most pronounced for at-the-money and out-of-the-money options. These options derive most or all of their value from the time remaining until expiration and the potential for favorable price movements in the underlying asset. As expiration nears, the likelihood of significant price movements decreases, causing these options to lose value rapidly. Liquidity risk is another factor to consider when trading options. While highly popular stocks and indices typically have liquid options markets, less popular underlyings may have wider bid-ask spreads and lower trading volumes. This can make it difficult to enter or exit positions at favorable prices, potentially increasing trading costs and impacting overall profitability.

The complexity of options strategies themselves can also be a source of risk. Many advanced options strategies involve multiple legs and complex payoff structures. While these strategies can be powerful tools when used correctly, they can also lead to unexpected outcomes if not fully understood. For instance, a trader might implement a strategy thinking it has limited risk, only to find that under certain market conditions, the risk is much greater than anticipated. Options trading also carries the risk of early assignment for American-style options. If you've sold options, there's always the possibility that the option buyer will exercise their right to buy or sell the underlying asset before expiration. This can disrupt your strategy and potentially lead to unexpected losses or tax consequences. Another risk to consider is the potential for option prices to be influenced by factors beyond just the price movement of the underlying asset. Corporate actions like stock splits, dividends, or mergers and acquisitions can have complex effects on option pricing and position outcomes. Traders need to be aware of these events and understand their potential impact on their options positions.

Given these risks, the importance of a comprehensive risk management plan cannot be overstated. A well-crafted risk management plan should address several key areas:

1) Position Sizing: Never risk more on a single trade than you can afford to lose. Many experienced options traders limit their exposure to any single position to a small percentage of their overall portfolio.

2) Diversification: Avoid concentrating too much of your portfolio in a single strategy or underlying asset. Diversification can help spread risk and potentially smooth out returns.

3) Stop-Loss Orders: Consider using stop-loss orders to automatically close out positions if losses reach a predetermined level. However, be aware that in fast-moving markets, stop-loss orders may not execute at the expected price.

4) Scenario Analysis: Before entering a trade, consider various potential outcomes. What's your maximum loss? What market conditions would lead to this loss? What's your plan if the trade moves against you?

5) Ongoing Education: The options market is constantly evolving. Commit to ongoing education to stay informed about new strategies, risk management techniques, and market dynamics.

6) Paper Trading: Before risking real money, consider paper trading to test your strategies and risk management approach in a simulated environment.

7) Monitoring and Adjustment: Regularly monitor your positions and be prepared to make adjustments as market conditions change. Don't simply set and forget options trades.

8) Use of Protective Strategies: Consider using strategies like stop-loss orders, collar strategies, or married puts to limit potential losses on your positions.

9) Understand Margin Requirements: If trading on margin, be fully aware of the margin requirements for your positions and how they might change in different market conditions.

10) Have an Exit Plan: Before entering a trade, know your criteria for exiting, both for taking profits and cutting losses. Stick to this plan to avoid emotional decision-making.

It's also crucial to understand your own risk tolerance and trading style. Options strategies that work well for one trader may be unsuitable for another due to differences in risk tolerance, trading goals, or available capital. Remember, while options can be used to reduce portfolio risk when used as a hedging tool, they can also significantly increase risk when used for speculation. Never trade options with money you can't afford to lose, and always ensure you fully understand the risk-reward profile of any strategy before implementing it. As we progress through this book and explore various options strategies, we'll continue to emphasize risk management. Each strategy has its own risk profile, and understanding these risks is just as important as understanding the potential rewards. By respecting the risks inherent in options trading and implementing robust risk management practices, you'll be better positioned to harness the power of options while protecting your capital.

Setting Up Your Trading Account

The foundation of successful options trading begins with selecting the right brokerage and setting up an appropriate trading account. This process involves more than just finding the lowest commissions; it requires careful consideration of various factors to ensure you have the tools, resources, and support needed to execute your trading strategies effectively. Choosing a brokerage is a crucial first step in your options trading journey. The right brokerage can provide you with the necessary tools, education, and support to help you succeed, while the wrong choice can hinder your progress and potentially lead to costly mistakes. When evaluating brokerages, consider factors such as commissions and fees, platform features, research and educational resources, customer support, and the types of trades and strategies they allow.

Commissions and fees are often the first things traders look at when choosing a brokerage, and for good reason. Options trading can involve frequent transactions, and high commissions can quickly eat into your profits. Many brokerages now offer commission-free stock and ETF trades, but options trades usually still incur per-contract fees. Look for brokerages that offer competitive pricing on options trades, but don't let this be your only consideration. The trading platform provided by the brokerage is another crucial factor. A good platform should be intuitive and easy to use, with real-time data, charting tools, and the ability to quickly execute complex options strategies. Some brokerages offer web-based platforms, desktop software, and mobile apps, allowing you to trade from anywhere. Consider which of these are important to you and test out the platforms if possible. Many brokerages offer demo accounts that allow you to explore their platform before committing.

Research and educational resources can be particularly valuable for options traders, especially those just starting out. Look for brokerages that offer comprehensive educational materials, including articles, videos, webinars, and even live training sessions. Some brokerages also provide advanced research tools, including options-specific screeners, probability calculators, and strategy builders. These tools can be invaluable in helping you identify potential trades and analyze their risk-reward profiles. Customer support is another important consideration, particularly for new traders who may need assistance navigating the complexities of options trading. Look for brokerages that offer multiple support channels, including phone, email, and live chat. Some brokerages even offer dedicated support lines for options traders. Consider the hours of availability as well, especially if you plan to trade outside of regular market hours. It's also important to consider the types of trades and strategies the brokerage allows. Some brokerages restrict certain high-risk strategies, such as naked option selling, to more experienced traders or those with larger account balances. If you're interested in advanced strategies, make sure the brokerage you choose will allow you to implement them.

Once you've chosen a brokerage, the next step is to decide on the type of account you need. The most common account types for individual traders are cash accounts and margin accounts. A cash account requires you to have the full amount of any trade in the account at the time of execution. This limits your trading capabilities but also limits your risk. A margin account, on the other hand, allows you to borrow money from the brokerage to increase your buying power. This can be useful for certain options strategies, but it also increases your risk. With a margin account, you can potentially lose more than your initial investment. Most brokerages require a margin account for certain options strategies, particularly those involving short options positions.

For retirement savings, you might consider opening an IRA (Individual Retirement Account) that allows options trading. However, be aware that there are restrictions on the types of options strategies you can use in an IRA, and margin is generally not allowed. When opening an account, you'll need to meet certain requirements set by both the brokerage and regulatory bodies. These typically include minimum deposit requirements, which can range from zero to several thousand dollars depending on the brokerage and account type. You'll also need to provide personal information for identity verification purposes. Most brokerages will also require you to fill out an options agreement form. This form asks about your financial situation, investment experience, and trading objectives. Based on your responses, the brokerage will assign you an options trading level, which determines the types of options strategies you're approved to trade. Be honest when filling out this form; overstating your experience or financial situation to gain access to higher-level strategies can lead to increased risk and potential losses.

Once your account is set up, it's time to familiarize yourself with the tools and resources available to options traders. These can vary significantly between brokerages, but some common tools include:

1) Options Chain: This is a table showing all available option contracts for a particular underlying asset. It typically includes information such as strike prices, expiration dates, bid and ask prices, volume, and open interest.

2) Strategy Builder: This tool allows you to construct complex options strategies and visualize their potential outcomes. It can be particularly useful for understanding the risk-reward profile of multi-leg strategies.

3) Probability Calculator: This tool uses current market data to estimate the likelihood of an option expiring in-the-money or reaching a specific price by expiration.

4) Greeks Calculator: This helps you understand how changes in various factors (such as underlying price,

time to expiration, and implied volatility) might affect the price of an option.

5) Options Screener: This tool allows you to filter options contracts based on specific criteria, helping you identify potential trading opportunities.

6) Paper Trading: Many brokerages offer paper trading accounts that allow you to practice trading strategies with virtual money. This can be an excellent way to gain experience without risking real capital.

7) Risk Management Tools: These might include features like position sizing calculators, portfolio analysis tools, and risk graphs that visualize the potential outcomes of your trades.

8) Market Data and News: Access to real-time market data, news feeds, and economic calendars can help you stay informed about events that might impact your trades.

9) Educational Resources: Look for brokerages that offer comprehensive educational materials, including articles, videos, webinars, and even live training sessions.

10) Mobile Trading Apps: In today's fast-paced markets, the ability to monitor and manage your trades on the go can be crucial.

As you set up your account and explore these tools, remember that they are just that - tools. They can provide valuable information and insights, but they don't guarantee success. It's crucial to develop a solid understanding of options trading principles and to use these tools to support your decision-making process, not to replace it.

Also, be aware that the availability and sophistication of these tools can vary significantly between brokerages. Some may offer advanced features like back-testing capabilities or integration with external analysis software, while others may provide more basic functionality. Consider which tools are most important for your trading style and strategy when choosing a brokerage. Finally, don't underestimate the importance of ongoing education and practice. Options trading is complex, and the markets are constantly evolving. Many brokerages offer ongoing educational resources, including webinars, articles, and even one-on-one coaching sessions. Take advantage of these resources to continually improve your knowledge and skills. Remember, setting up your trading account is just the beginning of your options trading journey. It's the foundation upon which you'll build your trading career. Take the time to choose the right brokerage, set up your account properly, and familiarize yourself with the available tools and resources. This initial investment of time and effort can pay significant dividends as you progress in your options trading endeavors.

Chapter Two

Essential Strategies for Beginners

"The journey of a thousand miles begins with one step."
- Lao Tzu

The Long Call

As we venture deeper into the world of options trading, it's crucial to start with the fundamental strategies that form the building blocks of more complex approaches. In this chapter, we'll explore several essential strategies that are particularly well-suited for beginners. These strategies offer a balance of potential reward and manageable risk, making them ideal starting points for those new to options trading. We'll begin with one of the most basic and widely used options strategies: the long call.

The long call strategy is often the first options strategy that new traders learn, and for good reason. It's straightforward to understand, has limited risk, and offers the potential for significant gains. At its core, a long call position is created when a trader buys a call option, giving them the right, but not the obligation, to buy the underlying asset at a specific price (the strike price) before or at a specific date (the expiration date). The basic mechanics of a long call are relatively simple. When you buy a call option, you're essentially making a bullish bet on the underlying asset. If the price of the underlying asset rises above the strike price plus the premium paid for the option, you start to profit. Your potential profit is theoretically unlimited, as it grows with each dollar the underlying asset moves above your breakeven point. On the other hand, your risk is limited to the premium you paid for the option. If the underlying asset's price doesn't rise above the strike price by expiration, your option will expire worthless, and you'll lose the entire premium. One of the key advantages of the long call strategy is the leverage it provides. For a relatively small upfront cost (the option premium), you gain exposure to a much larger position in the underlying asset. This leverage can amplify your returns if your prediction is correct. For example, if you buy a call option on a stock trading at $100 with a strike price of $105 for a premium of $3, and the stock rises to $110 by expiration, your option would be worth at least $5 (the difference between the stock price and the strike price). This represents a 66% return on your investment, while the stock itself only increased by 10%.

The long call strategy is particularly useful in several scenarios. First and foremost, it's an excellent way to benefit from an anticipated rise in the price of the underlying asset. If you believe a stock, index, or other asset is likely to increase in value, buying a call option allows you to profit from this movement without having to commit the capital required to buy the asset outright. Long calls can also be used as a way to limit risk when entering a bullish position. Instead of buying shares of a stock, which exposes you to the full downside risk if the stock price falls, buying a call option limits your risk to the premium paid. This can be particularly useful in volatile markets or when you're not completely confident in your bullish outlook.

Another scenario where long calls can be valuable is when you're expecting a significant event that could drive up the price of the underlying asset. This could be an earnings report, a product launch, or any other event that you believe will have a positive impact on the asset's value. The leverage provided by options can allow you to potentially profit significantly from such events while limiting your downside risk. Long calls can also be used as part of more complex strategies. For example, they can be combined with long puts to create a long straddle strategy, which profits from large price movements in either direction. They can also be used in conjunction with stock ownership in covered call writing, a popular income-generating strategy.

Now, let's walk through the step-by-step process of executing a long call strategy:

1) Identify the Underlying Asset: The first step is to choose the asset you believe will increase in value. This could be a stock, an ETF, an index, or any other asset that has options available. This decision should be based on thorough research and analysis. Consider factors such as the asset's historical performance, current market conditions, upcoming events that could impact the asset's price, and any relevant economic indicators.

2) Determine Your Price Target and Timeframe: Based on your analysis, decide how much you expect the asset's price to increase and over what period. This will help you choose the appropriate strike price and expiration date. Be realistic in your expectations; while options can provide significant leverage, they require the underlying asset to move in your favor within a specific time frame to be profitable.

3) Select the Strike Price: Choose a strike price based on your price target and risk tolerance. An at-the-money option (where the strike price is close to the current asset price) offers a balance of cost and potential profit. An out-of-the-money option (with a strike price above the current asset price) is cheaper but requires a larger price move to be profitable. In-the-money options (with a strike price below the current asset price) are more expensive but have a higher probability of being profitable at expiration.

4) Choose the Expiration Date: Select an expiration date that gives your prediction enough time to play out. Longer-dated options are more expensive but provide more time for the asset price to move in your favor. However, they're also more affected by time decay, especially in the last month before expiration. Shorter-dated options are cheaper but give you less time for your prediction to come true. Consider any upcoming events

that could impact the asset's price when choosing your expiration date.

5) Determine Position Size: Decide how many contracts to buy based on your risk tolerance and the amount of capital you're willing to allocate to the trade. Remember, each options contract typically represents 100 shares of the underlying asset. It's generally advisable to start small when you're new to options trading. Many experienced traders suggest risking no more than 1-2% of your total trading capital on any single trade.

6) Place the Order: Using your brokerage platform, place an order to buy the call option. You can typically choose between a market order (which executes immediately at the best available price) or a limit order (which only executes if you can get a specified price or better). For less liquid options, limit orders are often preferred to ensure you don't overpay due to a wide bid-ask spread.

7) Monitor the Position: Once your order is filled, keep an eye on the position. The value of your option will fluctuate based on changes in the underlying asset's price, time decay, and changes in implied volatility. Be prepared for the possibility of significant price swings, as options can be quite volatile.

8) Plan Your Exit: Decide in advance at what profit level you'll sell the option, or at what loss level you'll cut your

position. Having a plan can help you avoid making emotional decisions. Some traders use a specific profit target, such as 50% or 100% of the premium paid. Others might use technical indicators or changes in the underlying asset's price as signals to exit the trade.

9) Close the Position: To realize your profit or limit your loss, you'll need to sell the option before expiration. Alternatively, if the option is in-the-money at expiration, you might choose to exercise it to buy the underlying asset. Be aware that most options are not exercised but are instead closed out by selling them before expiration.

While the long call strategy can be highly rewarding, it's important to be aware of its risks and limitations. Time decay works against long option positions, eroding their value as expiration approaches. This means that even if the underlying asset price doesn't move, you can lose money on the position. The rate of time decay accelerates as expiration nears, which is why many options traders avoid holding long options into the last few weeks before expiration unless they have a strong conviction about an impending price move. Additionally, options are sensitive to changes in implied volatility. A decrease in implied volatility can negatively impact the value of your long call, even if the underlying asset price moves in your favor. This is why it's important to consider the current level of implied volatility when entering a long call position. Buying options when implied volatility is high can be risky, as a subsequent decrease in volatility could offset any gains from favorable price movement in the underlying asset.

It's also crucial to remember that options are complex instruments, and their value doesn't always move in a straightforward manner with the underlying asset. Factors like time to expiration, implied volatility, and the option's delta all play a role in determining its price. As such, it's important to thoroughly understand these factors before implementing a long call strategy. One way to mitigate some of the risks associated with long calls is to consider using spreads. For example, a bull call spread involves buying a call option at one strike price while simultaneously selling a call option at a higher strike price. This reduces both the cost and the potential profit of the position, but it also reduces the impact of time decay and changes in implied volatility.

Another important consideration when using long calls is the impact of dividends. If you're buying calls on a dividend-paying stock, be aware that the stock price typically drops by the amount of the dividend on the ex-dividend date. This can negatively impact the value of your call option, especially if the ex-dividend date falls just before the option's expiration. It's also worth noting that long calls can be used as a stock replacement strategy. Instead of buying shares of a stock outright, you could buy deep in-the-money calls. This strategy provides similar exposure to the stock's price movements but requires less capital and limits your downside risk. However, it also means you won't receive any dividends the stock might pay, and you'll need to manage the position more actively due to the option's time decay.

When implementing a long call strategy, it's important to consider the overall market environment. In a strong bull market, long calls on broad market indices or leading stocks can be particularly effective. However, in a bear market or a period of high volatility, the risks associated with long calls increase. In such environments, more conservative strategies or put options might be more appropriate. As you gain experience with long calls, you'll develop a better sense of when to use them and how to manage the positions effectively. You might find that certain sectors or types of stocks tend to work better for long call strategies. For example, growth stocks or stocks with upcoming catalysts often provide good opportunities for long calls. It's also important to keep detailed records of your trades. Track not only your profits and losses but also the reasons for entering and exiting each trade. This will help you refine your strategy over time and identify any patterns in your trading that need improvement.

In conclusion, the long call is a fundamental options strategy that offers the potential for significant profits with limited risk. It's an excellent starting point for beginners in options trading, providing a straightforward way to benefit from anticipated price increases in an underlying asset. However, like all trading strategies, it requires careful analysis, risk management, and a solid understanding of options mechanics to be used effectively. As you become more comfortable with long calls, you can start to explore how they can be combined with other options or stock positions to create more sophisticated strategies. For example, you might use long calls as part of a covered call strategy, or combine them with put options to create straddles or strangles. Remember, successful options trading is not just about picking the right direction of the underlying asset. It's about choosing the right strategy for your market outlook, managing your positions effectively, and continually educating yourself about the intricacies of options. With practice and experience, you'll be better prepared to explore more complex options strategies and to use options as part of a comprehensive trading or investing approach.

The Long Put

Just as the long call strategy allows traders to profit from anticipated price increases, the long put strategy provides a way to benefit from expected price declines. The long put is another fundamental options strategy that's particularly useful for beginners to understand and implement. It offers a way to profit from bearish market movements while limiting risk, making it an essential tool in any options trader's toolkit. This strategy is not only valuable for speculative purposes but also serves as a crucial instrument for portfolio protection and risk management.

At its core, a long put position is created when a trader buys a put option. This gives the holder the right, but not the obligation, to sell the underlying asset at a specific price (the strike price) before or at a specific date (the expiration date). The long put is essentially a bearish strategy, allowing traders to profit from a decline in the price of the underlying asset. It's important to note that while the strategy is bearish in nature, it doesn't necessarily mean the trader wants the underlying asset to decline. In many cases, long puts are used as a form of insurance against potential losses in a portfolio.

The basic mechanics of a long put are relatively straightforward. When you buy a put option, you're making a bearish bet on the underlying asset. If the price of the underlying asset falls below the strike price minus the premium paid for the option, you start to profit. Your potential profit is substantial but limited, as it grows with each dollar the underlying asset moves below your breakeven point, until the asset price reaches zero. On the other hand, your risk is limited to the premium you paid for the option. If the underlying asset's price doesn't fall below the strike price by expiration, your option will expire worthless, and you'll lose the entire premium. This limited risk profile is one of the key attractions of the long put strategy, particularly for traders who are wary of the unlimited risk associated with short selling stocks. One of the key advantages of the long put strategy is the protection it offers. For a relatively small upfront cost (the option premium), you can hedge against potential losses in an underlying asset you own, or profit from a decline in an asset you don't own. This makes long puts a versatile tool for both hedging and speculative purposes. The leverage provided by options means that a relatively small move in the underlying asset can result in a significant percentage gain in the option's value, allowing traders to potentially realize substantial profits with a limited initial investment.

The long put strategy is particularly useful in several scenarios. First and foremost, it's an excellent way to profit from an anticipated decline in the price of the underlying asset. If you believe a stock, index, or other asset is likely to decrease in value, buying a put option allows you to profit from this movement without having to short sell the asset, which can be riskier and may not be possible in all account types. This is especially valuable in markets where short selling is restricted or in situations where borrowing costs for short selling are prohibitively high. Long puts are also commonly used as a hedging tool. If you own shares of a stock and are concerned about potential short-term downside, buying put options can provide protection. This strategy, known as a protective put, limits your potential losses while allowing you to participate in any upside if the stock price increases. It's essentially a form of portfolio insurance. Institutional investors and portfolio managers often use this strategy to protect large positions or entire portfolios against market downturns. The cost of the put options can be viewed as a premium paid for this insurance, much like you would pay for car or home insurance.

Another scenario where long puts can be valuable is when you're expecting a significant event that could drive down the price of the underlying asset. This could be an earnings report, a regulatory decision, or any other event that you believe will have a negative impact on the asset's value. The leverage provided by options can allow you to potentially profit significantly from such events while limiting your upside risk. This event-driven approach to options trading can be particularly effective when combined with thorough fundamental and technical analysis. Long puts can also be used as part of more complex strategies. For example, they can be combined with long calls to create a long straddle strategy, which profits from large price movements in either direction. They can also be used in conjunction with other options positions to create various spread strategies. As traders become more experienced, they often find that combining long puts with other options or stock positions can create strategies tailored to very specific market outlooks or risk profiles.

When considering a long put strategy, the first step is to identify the underlying asset you believe will decrease in value. This could be a stock, an ETF, an index, or any other asset that has options available. This decision should be based on thorough research and analysis. Consider factors such as the asset's historical performance, current market conditions, upcoming events that could impact the asset's price, and any relevant economic indicators. It's crucial to have a well-founded thesis for why you expect the asset's price to decline, rather than simply guessing or following market rumors. Once you've identified the underlying asset, you need to determine your price target and timeframe. Based on your analysis, decide how much you expect the asset's price to decrease and over what period. This will help you choose the appropriate strike price and expiration date. Be realistic in your expectations; while options can provide significant leverage, they require the underlying asset to move in your favor within a specific time frame to be profitable. It's often helpful to use technical analysis tools, such as support and resistance levels or moving averages, to help identify potential price targets.

Selecting the right strike price is a crucial decision in implementing a long put strategy. The strike price you choose will depend on your price target and risk tolerance. An at-the-money option (where the strike price is close to the current asset price) offers a balance of cost and potential profit. An out-of-the-money option (with a strike price below the current asset price) is cheaper but requires a larger price move to be profitable. In-the-money options (with a strike price above the current asset price) are more expensive but have a higher probability of being profitable at expiration. Your choice of strike price will affect not only the cost of the option but also its sensitivity to price movements in the underlying asset and its likelihood of being profitable at expiration.

The expiration date is another critical factor to consider. You need to select an expiration date that gives your prediction enough time to play out. Longer-dated options are more expensive but provide more time for the asset price to move in your favor. However, they're also more affected by time decay, especially in the last month before expiration. Shorter-dated options are cheaper but give you less time for your prediction to come true. Consider any upcoming events that could impact the asset's price when choosing your expiration date. It's often a good idea to choose an expiration date that's a bit further out than you think you'll need, to give your trade some extra time to work out. Determining the right position size is crucial for managing risk in options trading. Decide how many contracts to buy based on your risk tolerance and the amount of capital you're willing to allocate to the trade. Remember, each option contract typically represents 100 shares of the underlying asset. It's generally advisable to start small when you're new to options trading. Many experienced traders suggest risking no more than 1-2% of your total trading capital on any single trade. This helps to ensure that no single trade can have a catastrophic impact on your overall trading account.

When you're ready to place your trade, you'll need to decide between a market order and a limit order. A market order executes immediately at the best available price, while a limit order only executes if you can get a specified price or better. For less liquid options, limit orders are often preferred to ensure you don't overpay due to a wide bid-ask spread. It's important to be patient when using limit orders, as getting filled at the right price can have a significant impact on the profitability of your trade. Once your order is filled, it's crucial to monitor your position closely. The value of your option will fluctuate based on changes in the underlying asset's price, time decay, and changes in implied volatility. Be prepared for the possibility of significant price swings, as options can be quite volatile. Many traders use options Greeks, such as delta, gamma, theta, and vega, to help them understand how their position might change under various market conditions.

Having a clear exit plan is essential for successful options trading. Decide in advance at what profit level you'll sell the option, or at what loss level you'll cut your position. Having a plan can help you avoid making emotional decisions. Some traders use a specific profit target, such as 50% or 100% of the premium paid. Others might use technical indicators or changes in the underlying asset's price as signals to exit the trade. Whatever method you choose, it's important to stick to your plan and not let emotions drive your decision-making. To realize your profit or limit your loss, you'll need to sell the option before expiration. Alternatively, if the option is in-the-money at expiration, you might choose to exercise it to sell the underlying asset (if you own it) or settle in cash (if you don't). Be aware that most options are not exercised but are instead closed out by selling them before expiration. It's generally advisable to close out your position before expiration to avoid any complications that can arise from automatic exercise or assignment.

While the long put strategy can be highly effective, it's important to be aware of its risks and limitations. Like all long options positions, long puts are subject to time decay, which erodes their value as expiration approaches. This means that even if the underlying asset price doesn't move, you can lose money on the position. The rate of time decay accelerates as expiration nears, which is why many options traders avoid holding long options into the last few weeks before expiration unless they have a strong conviction about an impending price move. Additionally, options are sensitive to changes in implied volatility. A decrease in implied volatility can negatively impact the value of your long put, even if the underlying asset price moves in your favor. This is why it's important to consider the current level of implied volatility when entering a long put position. Buying options when implied volatility is high can be risky, as a subsequent decrease in volatility could offset any gains from favorable price movement in the underlying asset.

It's also crucial to remember that options are complex instruments, and their value doesn't always move in a straightforward manner with the underlying asset. Factors like time to expiration, implied volatility, and the option's delta all play a role in determining its price. As such, it's important to thoroughly understand these factors before implementing a long put strategy. Many traders spend considerable time studying options theory and practicing with paper trading accounts before risking real money on options trades. One way to mitigate some of the risks associated with long puts is to consider using spreads. For example, a bear put spread involves buying a put option at one strike price while simultaneously selling a put option at a lower strike price. This reduces both the cost and the potential profit of the position, but it also reduces the impact of time decay and changes in implied volatility. Spread strategies can be an excellent way for traders to fine-tune their risk-reward profile and potentially improve their odds of success.

When using long puts, it's important to be aware of potential corporate actions that could affect the underlying stock. For example, if a company announces a special dividend, the stock price typically drops by the amount of the dividend on the ex-dividend date. This could benefit your long put position, but it's important to understand how such events can impact option prices. Similarly, other corporate actions like stock splits, mergers, or acquisitions can have complex effects on option prices and positions. Long puts can also be used as part of a married put strategy, where you simultaneously buy shares of a stock and a put option on that stock. This strategy provides downside protection similar to a protective put, but it's implemented at the time of purchasing the stock rather than as a hedge on an existing position. This can be an effective way to establish a new stock position while immediately putting a floor under potential losses.

As you gain experience with long puts, you'll develop a better sense of when to use them and how to manage the positions effectively. You might find that certain market conditions or types of stocks tend to work better for long put strategies. For example, stocks with high valuations or companies facing significant challenges might provide good opportunities for long puts. Some traders focus on specific sectors or industries where they have particular expertise, allowing them to better identify potential opportunities for profitable put trades. It's also important to keep detailed records of your trades. Track not only your profits and losses but also the reasons for entering and exiting each trade. This will help you refine your strategy over time and identify any patterns in your trading that need improvement. Many successful options traders maintain detailed trading journals where they record not just the mechanical details of their trades, but also their thought processes, emotions, and lessons learned from each trade.

The long put is a fundamental options strategy that offers the potential for significant profits with limited risk when you anticipate a decline in the price of an underlying asset. It's an excellent tool for both speculation and hedging, providing a straightforward way to benefit from or protect against anticipated price decreases. However, like all trading strategies, it requires careful analysis, risk management, and a solid understanding of options mechanics to be used effectively. As you become more comfortable with long puts, you can start to explore how they can be combined with other options or stock positions to create more sophisticated strategies. For example, you might use long puts as part of a collar strategy, or combine them with call options to create straddles or strangles. The possibilities are nearly endless, and many traders spend years refining their approach to options trading.

Remember, successful options trading is not just about picking the right direction of the underlying asset. It's about choosing the right strategy for your market outlook, managing your positions effectively, and continually educating yourself about the intricacies of options. With practice and experience, you'll be better prepared to explore more complex options strategies and to use options as part of a comprehensive trading or investing approach. In conclusion, the long put strategy is a powerful tool in the options trader's arsenal. Whether used for speculation, hedging, or as part of more complex strategies, long puts offer a unique combination of limited risk and potentially significant profits. As with any financial instrument, it's crucial to approach long puts with a solid understanding of their mechanics, a well-thought-out trading plan, and a commitment to ongoing education and improvement. With these elements in place, long puts can be a valuable addition to your trading toolkit, helping you navigate both bull and bear markets with greater flexibility and control over your risk.

Covered Call Writing

Covered call writing is a popular options strategy that combines stock ownership with the sale of call options against that stock position. This strategy is often considered one of the more conservative options strategies, making it an excellent starting point for investors looking to generate additional income from their stock holdings or to potentially enhance their overall portfolio returns. Covered call writing is widely used by both individual investors and institutional money managers as a way to potentially boost portfolio yield and manage risk. Its popularity stems from its relative simplicity, lower risk profile compared to many other options strategies, and its potential to generate consistent income.

At its core, a covered call position is created when an investor owns shares of a stock and sells call options on that same stock. The term "covered" refers to the fact that the call options are backed by the underlying stock position, which limits the potential risk of the strategy. For each standard call option contract sold, the investor must own 100 shares of the underlying stock. This creates a balanced position where any potential obligation to deliver shares (if the call options are exercised) is "covered" by the existing stock holding. This aspect of the strategy is crucial, as it distinguishes covered calls from naked call writing, which involves selling call options without owning the underlying stock and can expose the investor to theoretically unlimited risk.

The basic mechanics of covered call writing are straightforward. When you sell a call option, you're giving someone else the right to buy your shares at a specific price (the strike price) before or at a specific date (the expiration date). In exchange for this right, you receive a premium, which is the price of the option. This premium represents immediate income for your portfolio. If the stock price remains below the strike price at expiration, the option expires worthless, and you keep both the premium and your shares. If the stock price rises above the strike price, the option may be exercised, and you would be obligated to sell your shares at the strike price. It's important to note that while you're obligated to sell at the strike price if the option is exercised, you still benefit from any price appreciation up to the strike price, in addition to keeping the option premium.

One of the key advantages of the covered call strategy is the income it generates. The premium received from selling the call option provides an additional source of return, over and above any dividends the stock might pay. This can be particularly attractive in low-yield environments or for investors seeking to generate regular income from their portfolio. The income from call premiums can help offset potential losses if the stock price declines, providing a small measure of downside protection. For example, if you own a stock trading at $50 and sell a call option with a $52 strike price for a $1 premium, you've effectively created a 2% yield ($1/$50) from the option premium alone, in addition to any dividend the stock might pay. Covered call writing is particularly useful in several scenarios. First, it's an excellent strategy for stocks that you believe will remain relatively stable or experience modest growth. In this scenario, you can potentially earn income from both dividends and option premiums while still participating in some of the stock's upside potential. It's important to note, however, that the upside potential is limited to the strike price of the call option plus the premium received. This limitation on upside potential is one of the main trade-offs of the covered call strategy.

Another scenario where covered calls can be valuable is when you're looking to potentially exit a stock position at a specific price. By selling call options at your target exit price, you can earn premium income while you wait for the stock to reach that level. If the stock rises to your target price and the calls are exercised, you've achieved your exit goal while earning additional income along the way. This can be an effective way to enhance returns on a position you're planning to sell anyway. Covered calls can also be used as a way to potentially lower the effective purchase price of a stock position. By consistently selling call options against your shares, you can gradually reduce your cost basis in the stock. Over time, this can significantly improve your overall return on the position, even if the stock price remains relatively stable. For instance, if you bought a stock at $50 and over the course of a year collected $3 in call premiums through multiple covered call trades, you've effectively reduced your cost basis to $47, improving your percentage return if you eventually sell the shares.

When considering implementing a covered call strategy, the first step is to select an appropriate stock. Ideally, you want to choose a stock that you're comfortable holding for the long term, as there's always the possibility that you'll need to keep the shares if the calls expire worthless. Look for stocks with relatively stable prices and potentially attractive dividend yields. Stocks with high implied volatility can offer higher option premiums, but they also come with increased risk of significant price movements. It's often beneficial to focus on blue-chip stocks or established companies in stable industries when starting out with covered call writing.

Once you've selected a stock, you need to decide on the strike price and expiration date for the call options you'll sell. The strike price you choose will depend on your outlook for the stock and your income goals. Selling options with a strike price close to the current stock price (at-the-money options) will generate more income but increases the likelihood that your shares will be called away. Selling options with a strike price further above the current stock price (out-of-the-money options) will generate less income but provides more potential for capital appreciation in the underlying stock. Your choice of strike price should reflect your expectations for the stock and your willingness to potentially sell at that price. The choice of expiration date is another important consideration. Shorter-term options (those expiring in 30 days or less) will generate income more frequently but require more active management of the position. Longer-term options (those expiring in 60 days or more) generate less frequent income but require less frequent trading and may have more favorable tax treatment in some jurisdictions. The choice of expiration date can also affect the amount of premium you receive, with longer-dated options generally offering higher premiums due to the greater time value.

When you're ready to execute the covered call strategy, you'll need to sell the call options through your brokerage platform. If you already own the underlying shares, you can simply sell the appropriate number of call contracts. If you don't yet own the shares, many brokers allow you to enter the stock purchase and option sale as a single transaction, often referred to as a "buy-write" order. This can be an efficient way to establish a covered call position in a single step. After establishing your covered call position, it's important to monitor it regularly. Keep an eye on the stock price relative to the strike price of your options, and be prepared for the possibility that your shares may be called away if the stock price rises above the strike price. Also, watch for any upcoming events, such as earnings reports or dividend payments, that could impact the stock price. These events can cause significant price movements and may affect the likelihood of your options being exercised.

As the expiration date approaches, you'll need to decide on your next steps. If the options are set to expire worthless, you might choose to sell new call options to generate additional income. This process of repeatedly selling call options against your stock position is sometimes referred to as a "rolling" strategy. If the options are in-the-money and likely to be exercised, you'll need to be prepared for the possibility of having your shares called away. Alternatively, you might choose to buy back the options before expiration to close out the position and retain your shares. This could be appropriate if you've captured most of the potential premium and want to avoid the risk of assignment, or if your outlook for the stock has become more bullish.

While covered call writing can be an effective strategy for generating income and potentially enhancing returns, it's important to be aware of its limitations and risks. The primary risk is that you may miss out on significant upside if the stock price rises sharply. Your gains are limited to the strike price plus the premium received, even if the stock price rises well above this level. This opportunity cost can be substantial in a strong bull market or if the underlying company experiences a significant positive event. Additionally, selling covered calls does not provide significant downside protection. While the premium received does slightly offset potential losses, you're still exposed to the full downside risk of owning the stock. If the stock price declines significantly, the income from the call premium may be small consolation. It's crucial to remember that covered call writing is primarily an income-generating strategy, not a hedge against major losses.

It's also important to consider the tax implications of covered call writing. In some jurisdictions, consistently selling covered calls may impact the tax treatment of your stock holdings. For example, it may affect the holding period for long-term capital gains treatment. In the United States, if you sell an in-the-money call option with more than 30 days to expiration, it may suspend the holding period of your stock for tax purposes. Always consult with a tax professional to understand the implications for your specific situation. Another factor to consider is the impact of dividends. If you sell call options with a strike price below the stock price minus the expected dividend, there's an increased likelihood that the options will be exercised just before the ex-dividend date. This is because the option holder may want to capture the dividend payment. If retaining your shares to capture dividends is important to you, be sure to consider this when selecting strike prices for your covered calls.

As you gain experience with covered call writing, you may want to explore more advanced variations of the strategy. For example, you might use a "rolling" technique, where you buy back the original options before expiration and simultaneously sell new options with a later expiration date. This can allow you to continue generating income while potentially avoiding having your shares called away. Some investors also use a technique called "laddering," where they sell call options at different strike prices or expiration dates to diversify their covered call positions. Another advanced technique is to combine covered call writing with protective puts, creating a strategy known as a "collar." This involves buying a put option while simultaneously selling a call option against your stock position. The collar strategy limits both your upside potential and downside risk, effectively creating a range within which your returns are constrained. This can be useful for protecting unrealized gains in a stock position while still generating some income through the call premium.

It's worth noting that covered call writing can be used on exchange-traded funds (ETFs) as well as individual stocks. This can be a way to generate income from broad market exposure or specific sector holdings. Some ETFs even implement covered call strategies internally, offering investors a way to access the strategy without having to manage the options positions themselves. When implementing a covered call strategy, it's crucial to have a clear understanding of your investment goals and risk tolerance. Are you primarily seeking income, or are you also hoping for capital appreciation? How much upside are you willing to forgo in exchange for the certainty of option premium income? How would you react if your shares were called away? Answering these questions can help you tailor your covered call approach to your specific needs and preferences.

It's also important to consider the overall market environment when implementing covered calls. In a strongly bullish market, covered calls may underperform simply holding the underlying stocks, as the strategy caps your upside. Conversely, in a flat or slightly bearish market, covered calls can outperform by providing additional income. Some investors adjust their covered call strategy based on their market outlook, selling closer-to-the-money calls when they expect minimal price appreciation and further out-of-the-money calls when they anticipate more significant gains. As with any investment strategy, education and practice are key to successful covered call writing. Many investors start by paper trading covered calls to get a feel for the mechanics and outcomes of the strategy without risking real money. Most brokerage platforms offer virtual trading accounts that allow you to practice options strategies in a simulated environment. This can be an excellent way to gain confidence and refine your approach before implementing the strategy with your actual portfolio.

It's also beneficial to stay informed about factors that can affect options pricing, such as implied volatility. Higher implied volatility generally results in higher option premiums, which can make covered call writing more attractive. However, high implied volatility also suggests that the market expects significant price movements, which could increase the likelihood of your shares being called away or experiencing substantial price declines. Covered call writing is a versatile strategy that can be an excellent tool for generating income and potentially enhancing portfolio returns. Its relatively low-risk nature makes it an ideal starting point for investors looking to incorporate options into their portfolio management approach. However, like all investment strategies, it requires careful consideration of your investment goals, risk tolerance, and market outlook. With practice and experience, covered call writing can become a valuable part of your overall investment strategy, providing a way to potentially boost returns and generate regular income from your stock holdings. Whether you're a conservative investor looking to enhance the yield of your portfolio, or a more active trader seeking to optimize the returns of your stock positions, covered call writing offers a flexible and potentially rewarding approach to options trading.

Protective Puts

Protective puts are a fundamental options strategy that serves as a form of portfolio insurance. This strategy involves buying put options to protect an existing long stock position against potential downside risk. Protective puts are widely used by both individual investors and institutional portfolio managers as a means of managing risk and preserving capital. The strategy is particularly valuable for those who want to maintain their stock positions while gaining some protection against market volatility or unexpected negative events.

At its core, a protective put position is created when an investor who owns shares of a stock purchases put options on that same stock. For each standard put option contract purchased, the investor typically protects 100 shares of the underlying stock. The put option gives the investor the right, but not the obligation, to sell their shares at a specific price (the strike price) before or at a specific date (the expiration date). This right acts as a safety net, limiting the potential losses on the stock position to a known amount, regardless of how far the stock price might fall. The basic mechanics of protective puts are straightforward. When you buy a put option, you're essentially purchasing insurance for your stock position. If the stock price remains above the strike price of the put option, your stock position continues to appreciate in value, and the put option simply expires worthless. However, if the stock price falls below the strike price, the put option increases in value, offsetting some or all of the losses in the stock position. In the worst-case scenario, where the stock price falls dramatically, your losses are limited to the difference between the stock price at the time you purchased the put and the strike price of the put, plus the cost of the put option premium.

One of the key advantages of the protective put strategy is the peace of mind it provides. By implementing this strategy, investors can potentially protect themselves against significant losses while still participating in the upside potential of their stock holdings. This can be particularly valuable during times of market uncertainty or when an investor has a large, unrealized gain in a stock position that they want to protect. Protective puts are particularly useful in several scenarios. First, they can be an excellent tool for managing risk in a portfolio. If you have a significant portion of your portfolio invested in a single stock or sector, protective puts can help limit your downside risk without forcing you to sell your shares and potentially incur capital gains taxes. This can be especially important for executives who hold large positions in their company's stock, or for investors who have inherited significant stock positions.

Another scenario where protective puts can be valuable is when you anticipate potential volatility or downside risk in the short term, but remain bullish on a stock over the long term. For example, if you own shares of a company that's about to report earnings, and you're concerned about a potential negative surprise, you could buy protective puts to guard against a sharp drop in the stock price. If the earnings report is positive and the stock rises, you've only lost the premium paid for the puts. But if the report is negative and the stock falls, your losses are limited.

Protective puts can also be used as part of a strategy to lock in unrealized gains on a stock position. If you've experienced significant appreciation in a stock but aren't ready to sell, perhaps due to tax considerations or because you believe there's still upside potential, protective puts allow you to establish a floor on your gains while still participating in any further upside. When considering implementing a protective put strategy, the first step is to determine how much protection you need. This will depend on factors such as your risk tolerance, the size of your stock position, and your outlook for the stock and the overall market. You'll need to balance the desire for protection against the cost of that protection, as put options can be expensive, especially during times of market uncertainty. Once you've decided on the level of protection you need, you'll need to choose the strike price and expiration date for your put options. The strike price you select will determine the level at which your protection kicks in. Choosing a strike price close to the current stock price will provide more complete protection but will be more expensive. Selecting a lower strike price will be cheaper but will provide protection only against more significant declines.

The choice of expiration date is another important consideration. Longer-dated options provide protection for a greater period but are more expensive. Shorter-dated options are cheaper but require more frequent renewal if you want ongoing protection. Some investors use a laddered approach, buying puts with different expiration dates to spread out the cost of protection over time. When you're ready to execute the protective put strategy, you'll need to purchase the put options through your brokerage platform. Be sure to buy puts for the correct underlying stock and in the appropriate quantity to protect your entire stock position. Many brokers offer tools to help you select the appropriate options based on your protection goals.

After establishing your protective put position, it's important to monitor it regularly. Keep an eye on the stock price relative to the strike price of your puts, and be prepared to adjust your strategy if market conditions change. For example, if the stock price rises significantly, you might consider selling your existing puts and buying new ones at a higher strike price to maintain your level of protection. As the expiration date of your puts approaches, you'll need to decide on your next steps. If the stock price has remained above the strike price, your puts will likely expire worthless, and you may want to consider purchasing new puts for continued protection. If the stock price has fallen below the strike price, you have several options. You could exercise the puts to sell your stock at the strike price, you could sell the puts to realize their value and offset some of your stock losses, or you could simply let the puts expire and sell your stock in the open market.

While protective puts can be an effective risk management tool, it's important to be aware of their limitations and costs. The primary drawback of protective puts is their cost. Put options can be expensive, especially for volatile stocks or during periods of market uncertainty. This ongoing cost can drag on your returns if the protection isn't needed. It's similar to paying for insurance – it's an expense you incur for protection you hope you'll never need to use. Additionally, while protective puts limit your downside risk, they don't eliminate it entirely. You can still lose money up to the strike price of the put, plus the cost of the put premium. For example, if you own a stock trading at $100 and buy a put with a strike price of $90 for $2, your maximum loss is $12 per share ($10 from stock decline to strike price plus $2 premium), which is still a significant potential loss.

It's also important to consider the tax implications of protective puts. In some jurisdictions, purchasing put options on a stock you own can affect the holding period of the stock for tax purposes. This could potentially impact your eligibility for long-term capital gains treatment. Always consult with a tax professional to understand the implications for your specific situation. Another factor to consider is the impact of dividends. If you're using protective puts on a dividend-paying stock, remember that put options don't entitle you to dividend payments. You'll continue to receive dividends on your stock holdings, but the put options themselves don't provide any dividend income.

As you gain experience with protective puts, you may want to explore more advanced variations of the strategy. For example, some investors use a "collar" strategy, which involves buying protective puts while simultaneously selling call options against their stock position. This can help offset the cost of the puts but caps the potential upside of the stock position. Another advanced technique is using index puts to hedge a diversified stock portfolio. Instead of buying puts on individual stocks, you could purchase puts on a broad market index to protect against overall market declines. This can be more cost-effective than buying puts on multiple individual stocks, especially for larger portfolios. It's worth noting that while protective puts are typically used with individual stocks, they can also be applied to exchange-traded funds (ETFs) or other securities that have options available. This can allow you to protect positions in specific sectors or asset classes.

When implementing a protective put strategy, it's crucial to have a clear understanding of your risk tolerance and investment goals. How much downside are you willing to accept? How much are you willing to pay for protection? How would a significant decline in your stock holdings impact your overall financial situation? Answering these questions can help you tailor your protective put approach to your specific needs and circumstances. It's also important to consider the overall market environment when implementing protective puts. In a strongly bullish market, the ongoing cost of put protection can be a drag on performance. Conversely, in a volatile or bearish market, the peace of mind and downside protection provided by puts may be well worth their cost. Some investors adjust their use of protective puts based on their market outlook, using them more extensively when they perceive increased market risk.

As with any option strategy, education and practice are key to successfully using protective puts. Many investors start by paper trading to get a feel for how protective puts work without risking real money. Most brokerage platforms offer virtual trading accounts that allow you to practice options strategies in a simulated environment. This can be an excellent way to gain confidence and refine your approach before implementing the strategy with your actual portfolio. It's also beneficial to stay informed about factors that can affect options pricing, such as implied volatility. Higher implied volatility generally results in more expensive put options, which can make protective puts more costly. However, periods of high implied volatility are often when protection is most valuable, so it's important to balance the cost of protection against the potential risks.

Protective puts are a valuable tool for managing risk in a stock portfolio. They offer a way to limit downside risk while still maintaining upside potential, providing a form of portfolio insurance that can help investors sleep better at night. However, like all investment strategies, protective puts require careful consideration of costs, benefits, and alternatives. They should be used as part of a comprehensive investment strategy that aligns with your goals, risk tolerance, and market outlook. Whether you're a conservative investor looking to protect against significant losses, or a more aggressive investor seeking to manage risk in a volatile stock position, protective puts offer a flexible and potentially powerful approach to risk management in your investment portfolio.

The Cash-Secured Put

The cash-secured put is a versatile options strategy that can serve multiple purposes for investors. It involves selling (or writing) put options while simultaneously setting aside enough cash to cover the potential purchase of the underlying stock.

This strategy is often used as an alternative method to acquire stocks at a lower price than their current market value, or as a way to generate income in a portfolio. The cash-secured put is considered a more conservative options strategy, making it suitable for investors who are comfortable with options but want to maintain a lower risk profile. At its core, a cash-secured put position is created when an investor sells a put option and sets aside enough cash to purchase the underlying stock if the option is exercised. For each standard put option contract sold, the investor must have enough cash to buy 100 shares of the underlying stock at the strike price. This cash requirement is what makes the put "secured" and distinguishes it from naked put writing, which can carry significantly more risk. The secured nature of this strategy means that the maximum loss is limited and known in advance, which is a key factor in its appeal to more conservative investors.

The basic mechanics of a cash-secured put are straightforward. When you sell a put option, you're giving someone else the right to sell you shares of the underlying stock at a specific price (the strike price) before or at a specific date (the expiration date). In exchange for taking on this obligation, you receive a premium, which is the price of the option. This premium represents immediate income for your portfolio. If the stock price remains above the strike price at expiration, the option expires worthless, and you keep the premium as profit. If the stock price falls below the strike price, you may be obligated to buy the shares at the strike price, effectively purchasing the stock at a discount to its price when you initially sold the put. One of the key advantages of the cash-secured put strategy is its potential to generate income while also providing an opportunity to acquire stocks at a lower price. The premium received from selling the put option provides immediate income, which can enhance portfolio returns. If the put is exercised and you end up purchasing the shares, you've essentially bought them at a discount equal to the strike price minus the premium received. This dual benefit of income generation and potential stock acquisition at a discount is what makes the cash-secured put strategy particularly attractive to many investors.

Cash-secured puts are particularly useful in several scenarios. First, they can be an excellent strategy for investors who want to buy a particular stock but believe it's currently overvalued. By selling a cash-secured put, you can potentially acquire the stock at a lower price while earning income in the meantime. If the stock doesn't fall to your desired purchase price, you still profit from the option premium. This scenario allows investors to be patient in their stock acquisition strategy while still generating returns. Another scenario where cash-secured puts can be valuable is when you're looking to generate income in a portfolio. In a low-yield environment, the premiums from selling puts can provide an alternative source of returns. This can be especially attractive for investors who are comfortable with the potential obligation to buy the underlying stocks. For retirees or others seeking regular income from their investments, cash-secured puts can be a useful tool to supplement dividend income or interest from bonds.

Cash-secured puts can also be used as part of a broader portfolio strategy. For example, they can be combined with covered calls in a strategy known as "The Wheel," where an investor alternates between selling cash-secured puts and covered calls on a stock they're willing to own long-term. This approach allows for consistent income generation while also providing opportunities for capital appreciation. When considering implementing a cash-secured put strategy, the first step is to select an appropriate stock. Ideally, you want to choose a stock that you're comfortable owning for the long term, as there's always the possibility that you'll end up purchasing the shares if the put is exercised. Look for stocks with solid fundamentals and a valuation that you believe represents good value at or below the current market price. It's crucial to conduct thorough research on the company, including its financial health, competitive position, and growth prospects. Remember, the goal is not just to generate income from option premiums, but potentially to become a shareholder in the company.

Once you've selected a stock, you need to decide on the strike price and expiration date for the put options you'll sell. The strike price you choose will depend on your target purchase price for the stock and your income goals. Selling puts with a strike price close to the current stock price will generate more income but increases the likelihood that you'll be obligated to buy the shares. Selling puts with a strike price further below the current stock price will generate less income but provides a larger potential discount if you end up purchasing the shares. Your choice of strike price should reflect both your assessment of the stock's fair value and your willingness to own the shares at that price.

The choice of expiration date is another important consideration. Shorter-term options (those expiring in 30 days or less) will allow you to generate income more frequently but require more active management of the position. Longer-term options (those expiring in 60 days or more) generate income less frequently but require less frequent trading and may have more favorable tax treatment in some jurisdictions. Your choice of expiration date should balance your desire for income, your willingness to actively manage the position, and your outlook for the stock over different time frames.

When you're ready to execute the cash-secured put strategy, you'll need to sell the put options through your brokerage platform. Be sure to have enough cash (or buying power) in your account to cover the potential purchase of shares. Many brokers will automatically hold this cash in reserve when you sell cash-secured puts. It's important to understand your broker's specific requirements and procedures for cash-secured puts before implementing this strategy. After establishing your cash-secured put position, it's important to monitor it regularly. Keep an eye on the stock price relative to the strike price of your options, and be prepared for the possibility that you may be obligated to buy the shares if the stock price falls below the strike price. Also, watch for any upcoming events, such as earnings reports or dividend announcements, that could impact the stock price. Stay informed about any news or developments related to the company or its industry that might affect the stock price.

As the expiration date approaches, you'll need to decide on your next steps. If the options are set to expire worthless (with the stock price above the strike price), you might choose to sell new put options to generate additional income. This process of repeatedly selling put options is sometimes referred to as "rolling" the position. If the stock price is below the strike price and the put is likely to be exercised, you'll need to be prepared to purchase the shares at the strike price. In some cases, you might choose to close out the position by buying back the put option before expiration, either to take profits or to avoid being assigned the shares. While cash-secured puts can be an effective strategy for generating income and potentially acquiring stocks at a discount, it's important to be aware of their limitations and risks. The primary risk is that you may be obligated to buy the stock at the strike price even if its market value has fallen significantly below that level. While you still benefit from the option premium, you could be left holding a stock position that's worth less than you paid for it. This risk is why it's crucial to only sell puts on stocks you're genuinely willing to own.

Additionally, by selling cash-secured puts, you're limiting your potential profit to the premium received. If the stock price rises significantly, you won't participate in that upside beyond keeping the premium. This opportunity cost can be substantial in a strong bull market. Some investors view this as a fair trade-off for the income and potential to acquire shares at a discount, but it's important to be aware of this limitation. It's also important to consider the tax implications of cash-secured puts. In some jurisdictions, the premiums received from selling puts may be treated as short-term capital gains, which are typically taxed at a higher rate than long-term capital gains. If you end up purchasing the stock, the premium received typically reduces your cost basis in the shares. This can affect your eventual capital gains or losses when you sell the shares. Always consult with a tax professional to understand the implications for your specific situation, as tax laws can be complex and vary by jurisdiction.

Another factor to consider is the impact of dividends. If you sell put options on a dividend-paying stock, remember that you won't receive any dividends unless you actually end up owning the shares. This opportunity cost should be factored into your decision-making process, especially if dividend income is an important part of your investment strategy. As you gain experience with cash-secured puts, you may want to explore more advanced variations of the strategy. For example, some investors use a "rolling" technique, where they buy back the original puts before expiration if the stock price has fallen, and simultaneously sell new puts with a later expiration date and possibly a lower strike price. This can allow you to avoid or delay having to purchase the shares while potentially generating additional income. However, it's important to note that rolling a position can also lock in a loss on the original put and may eventually lead to purchasing shares at a higher effective price than originally intended.

It's worth noting that while cash-secured puts are typically used with individual stocks, they can also be applied to exchange-traded funds (ETFs) or other securities that have options available. This can allow you to potentially acquire positions in specific sectors or asset classes at a discount. Using cash-secured puts on ETFs can be a way to implement this strategy with reduced single-stock risk, as ETFs provide built-in diversification. When implementing a cash-secured put strategy, it's crucial to have a clear understanding of your investment goals and risk tolerance. Are you primarily seeking income, or are you hoping to acquire shares of specific stocks? How would you react if you were obligated to purchase shares in a falling market? How much of your portfolio are you comfortable allocating to this strategy? Answering these questions can help you tailor your cash-secured put approach to your specific needs and preferences.

It's also important to consider the overall market environment when implementing cash-secured puts. In a strongly bullish market, you may find that your puts expire worthless more often, allowing you to generate consistent income but possibly missing out on significant stock appreciation. In a bearish market, you may end up purchasing stocks at prices that continue to decline. Some investors adjust their cash-secured put strategy based on their market outlook, selling puts on more defensive stocks during uncertain times and on more aggressive growth stocks during bullish periods. The level of implied volatility in the options market is another crucial factor to consider. Higher implied volatility generally results in higher option premiums, which can make selling cash-secured puts more attractive. However, high implied volatility also suggests that the market expects significant price movements, which could increase the likelihood of having the shares put to you. Some investors specifically seek out high volatility environments to sell puts, but this approach requires careful risk management.

As with any options strategy, education and practice are key to successful implementation of cash-secured puts. Many investors start by paper trading to get a feel for the mechanics and outcomes of the strategy without risking real money. Most brokerage platforms offer virtual trading accounts that allow you to practice options strategies in a simulated environment. This can be an excellent way to gain confidence and refine your approach before implementing the strategy with your actual portfolio. It's also beneficial to stay informed about factors that can affect options pricing, such as implied volatility, interest rates, and time decay. Understanding these factors can help you make more informed decisions about when to enter or exit positions, and how to adjust your strategy in different market conditions. Many successful options traders continually educate themselves about options theory and market dynamics to refine their approach.

When using cash-secured puts, it's important to diversify your positions. Avoid concentrating too much of your portfolio in a single stock or sector. Diversification can help manage risk and potentially improve overall returns. Some investors set rules for themselves, such as limiting the amount of capital allocated to cash-secured puts to a certain percentage of their overall portfolio. It's also crucial to have a plan for what to do if you're assigned shares. Will you hold the shares long-term? Sell covered calls against them? Sell them immediately? Having a clear plan can help you avoid making emotional decisions if you end up purchasing shares in a declining market. Remember that while cash-secured puts can be a powerful tool, they should be just one part of a broader investment strategy. They can complement other income-generating strategies, such as dividend investing or bond investing, and can be used alongside other options strategies to create a well-rounded approach to portfolio management.

Cash-secured puts are a versatile strategy that can be an excellent tool for generating income and potentially acquiring stocks at a discount. Their relatively conservative nature makes them an attractive option for investors looking to incorporate options into their portfolio management approach while maintaining a lower risk profile. However, like all investment strategies, they require careful consideration of your investment goals, risk tolerance, and market outlook. With practice and experience, cash-secured puts can become a valuable part of your overall investment strategy, providing a way to potentially enhance returns and acquire stock positions in a disciplined manner. Whether you're a conservative investor looking for additional income, or a more aggressive investor seeking to acquire stocks at a discount, cash-secured puts offer a flexible and potentially rewarding approach to options trading.

Chapter Three

Intermediate Strategies for Growing Traders

"Success is not final; failure is not fatal: It is the courage to continue that counts."
- Winston Churchill

As investors gain confidence and experience with basic options strategies, they often seek more sophisticated approaches to fine-tune their risk-reward profiles and capitalize on specific market outlooks. This chapter introduces intermediate options strategies that offer more nuanced ways to profit from market movements while often providing better risk management than simple long options positions. These strategies typically involve multiple options contracts, allowing traders to create custom payoff structures tailored to their market views and risk tolerance.

The Bull Call Spread

The bull call spread, also known as a long call spread or a debit call spread, is a popular options strategy that allows traders to profit from a bullish outlook on a stock or other underlying asset while limiting both potential profit and loss. This strategy involves simultaneously buying a call option at one strike price and selling another call option at a higher strike price, with both options having the same expiration date. The bull call spread is an excellent stepping stone for traders looking to move beyond basic long call positions, offering a more cost-effective way to implement a bullish view with defined risk. At its core, a bull call spread consists of two call options: one purchased and one sold. The trader buys a call option with a lower strike price and simultaneously sells a call option with a higher strike price. Both options have the same underlying asset and expiration date. The net cost of this position (the debit) is the difference between the premium paid for the long call and the premium received for the short call. This structure allows traders to reduce the cost of taking a bullish position compared to buying a call option outright, as the premium received from selling the higher strike call partially offsets the cost of the lower strike call purchased.

The mechanics of a bull call spread can be understood by breaking down the two components. The long call with the lower strike price gives you the right to buy the underlying asset at that strike price. As the stock price increases, this option gains value, providing the bullish exposure you're seeking. The short call with the higher strike price, which you sell, obligates you to sell the underlying asset at that higher strike price if the option is exercised. This short call caps your potential profit but reduces the cost of the strategy. The interplay between these two options creates a defined risk-reward profile that many traders find attractive. The maximum profit for a bull call spread is achieved when the underlying asset's price at expiration is at or above the higher strike price. In this scenario, both options are in-the-money, and the profit is the difference between the two strike prices minus the initial debit paid for the spread. The maximum loss, on the other hand, is limited to the initial debit paid for the spread, which occurs if the underlying asset's price at expiration is below the lower strike price, causing both options to expire worthless. This defined risk-reward profile is one of the key attractions of the bull call spread strategy.

Bull call spreads are particularly useful in several scenarios. When you have a moderate bullish outlook, expecting the underlying asset to rise but unsure about significant upside potential, a bull call spread allows you to profit from a moderate increase while limiting your risk. This can be especially valuable in markets where you anticipate steady growth rather than explosive moves. Additionally, in high volatility environments where options premiums are expensive, bull call spreads can provide a more cost-effective way to implement a bullish view compared to buying calls outright. The premium received from selling the higher strike call helps to offset the high cost of the lower strike call, making the strategy more accessible in these market conditions. Risk management is another key benefit of the bull call spread. If you want to limit your potential loss on a bullish trade, this strategy caps your maximum loss at the initial debit paid. This can be particularly appealing for traders who want to maintain strict control over their risk exposure or who are working with smaller accounts where large losses could be particularly detrimental. The defined maximum loss also makes it easier to size positions appropriately within a broader portfolio context.

Compared to a long call strategy, the bull call spread typically has a lower break-even point due to the premium received from selling the higher strike call. This means the underlying asset doesn't need to move as far in your favor for the trade to become profitable. For traders who prefer clearly defined maximum profit and loss scenarios, the bull call spread offers a straightforward risk-reward profile. This clarity can be valuable for both planning trades and managing ongoing positions. Implementing a bull call spread involves several key steps, beginning with thorough market analysis. Start by developing a bullish thesis on the underlying asset, considering both fundamental and technical factors that support your outlook. Determine your price target and the timeframe in which you expect the bullish move to occur. This analysis will inform your choice of strike prices and expiration date for the spread.

Once you've completed your analysis, select the underlying asset on which you want to implement the bull call spread. This could be an individual stock, an ETF, or even a market index, depending on your outlook and the available options. Choose an expiration date that aligns with your expected timeframe for the bullish move to occur. Remember that options with more time until expiration will be more expensive, but they also give your thesis more time to play out. Selecting the appropriate strike prices is a crucial decision in constructing your bull call spread. Choose the lower strike price for the call you'll buy and the higher strike price for the call you'll sell. The width between these strikes will determine your maximum profit potential. A wider spread (larger difference between strike prices) will increase both the potential profit and the cost of the spread. Conversely, a narrower spread will limit the potential profit but will be less expensive to implement. Your choice should reflect your specific price target and risk tolerance.

Determining the right position size is essential for effective risk management. Decide how many spreads to trade based on your risk tolerance and account size. Remember that each spread typically represents 100 shares of the underlying asset. It's generally advisable to limit the risk on any single trade to a small percentage of your overall account value. When you're ready to place the trade, enter the bull call spread as a single order, specifying both the buy and sell legs simultaneously. This ensures you get filled on both sides of the spread and avoids the risk of only partially completing the strategy. Most modern trading platforms allow you to enter spread orders directly, simplifying the process. However, it's still important to double-check all the details before submitting your order.

Before entering the trade, it's crucial to set a clear exit strategy. Determine in advance at what profit level you'll close the position and at what loss level you'll exit to limit your downside. Having predetermined exit points can help you avoid making emotional decisions in the heat of the moment. Some traders set profit targets at a certain percentage of the maximum potential gain, while others may look to technical levels on the chart of the underlying asset. Once the trade is executed, it's important to monitor and manage the position as it progresses. Keep track of how the spread's value changes in relation to movements in the underlying asset. Be prepared to adjust or close the trade as market conditions change or as you approach expiration. Some traders actively manage their spreads, potentially closing the position early if a significant portion of the maximum profit has been captured or if their outlook on the underlying asset changes.

When executing a bull call spread, it's crucial to consider the bid-ask spreads of both options. Wide spreads can significantly impact the cost and potential profitability of the strategy. Using limit orders can help ensure you enter the trade at a favorable price. In some cases, traders may choose to leg into the position by entering each side of the spread separately. While this approach can sometimes result in better fills, it carries the risk of adverse price movements between trades and should be attempted only by more experienced traders. It's also important to be aware of the potential for early assignment on the short call, especially if the underlying asset pays dividends. While early assignment is generally rare, it can occur if the short call becomes deeply in-the-money. Understanding the dynamics of early assignment and how to manage such situations is important for any trader using spread strategies.

The bull call spread offers traders a way to express a bullish view with defined risk and potentially lower cost compared to outright long calls. However, it's important to remember that this strategy caps your potential profit, which may be a significant drawback in strongly bullish markets. Traders must weigh this limitation against the benefits of reduced cost and defined risk when deciding whether a bull call spread is appropriate for a given situation. As with any options strategy, success with bull call spreads requires thorough understanding, careful planning, and disciplined execution. Traders should practice implementing these spreads in a paper trading account before risking real capital. Additionally, it's valuable to analyze the performance of your spreads over time, learning from both successful and unsuccessful trades to refine your approach. In conclusion, the bull call spread is a versatile and powerful tool in the options trader's arsenal. It provides a way to express a bullish outlook with defined risk and potentially lower cost than simple long call positions. By mastering this strategy, traders can expand their ability to profit from bullish market moves while maintaining better control over their risk exposure.

The Bear Put Spread

The bear put spread, also known as a long put spread or a debit put spread, is a popular options strategy that allows traders to profit from a bearish outlook on a stock or other underlying asset while limiting both potential profit and loss. This strategy is the bearish counterpart to the bull call spread and involves simultaneously buying a put option at one strike price and selling another put option at a lower strike price, with both options having the same expiration date. The bear put spread is an excellent tool for traders looking to implement a bearish view with defined risk and potentially lower cost compared to buying puts outright.

At its core, a bear put spread consists of two put options: one purchased and one sold. The trader buys a put option with a higher strike price and simultaneously sells a put option with a lower strike price. Both options have the same underlying asset and expiration date. The net cost of this position (the debit) is the difference between the premium paid for the long put and the premium received for the short put. This structure allows traders to reduce the cost of taking a bearish position compared to buying a put option outright, as the premium received from selling the lower strike put partially offsets the cost of the higher strike put purchased. The mechanics of a bear put spread can be understood by breaking down the two components. The long put with the higher strike price gives you the right to sell the underlying asset at that strike price. As the stock price decreases, this option gains value, providing the bearish exposure you're seeking. The short put with the lower strike price, which you sell, obligates you to buy the underlying asset at that lower strike price if the option is exercised. This short put caps your potential profit but reduces the cost of the strategy. The interplay between these two options creates a defined risk-reward profile that many traders find attractive, especially in bearish market conditions.

The maximum profit for a bear put spread is achieved when the underlying asset's price at expiration is at or below the lower strike price. In this scenario, both options are in-the-money, and the profit is the difference between the two strike prices minus the initial debit paid for the spread. The maximum loss, on the other hand, is limited to the initial debit paid for the spread, which occurs if the underlying asset's price at expiration is above the higher strike price, causing both options to expire worthless. This defined risk-reward profile is one of the key attractions of the bear put spread strategy, as it allows traders to precisely calculate their potential outcomes before entering the trade.

Bear put spreads are particularly useful in several scenarios. When you have a moderate bearish outlook, expecting the underlying asset to decline but unsure about significant downside potential, a bear put spread allows you to profit from a moderate decrease while limiting your risk. This can be especially valuable in markets where you anticipate steady declines rather than dramatic crashes. Additionally, in high volatility environments where options premiums are expensive, bear put spreads can provide a more cost-effective way to implement a bearish view compared to buying puts outright. The premium received from selling the lower strike put helps to offset the high cost of the higher strike put, making the strategy more accessible in these market conditions.

Risk management is another key benefit of the bear put spread. If you want to limit your potential loss on a bearish trade, this strategy caps your maximum loss at the initial debit paid. This can be particularly appealing for traders who want to maintain strict control over their risk exposure or who are working with smaller accounts where large losses could be particularly detrimental. The defined maximum loss also makes it easier to size positions appropriately within a broader portfolio context, allowing for more precise risk management. Bear put spreads can also be effectively used as a hedging tool. Investors with long stock positions or portfolios with significant market exposure can use bear put spreads to protect against potential downside moves. By implementing these spreads, traders can offset some of the losses that might occur in their long positions during market declines, while limiting the cost of this protection compared to buying puts outright. This makes bear put spreads a valuable tool for portfolio managers and individual investors alike who want to manage their overall market risk.

Implementing a bear put spread involves several key steps, beginning with thorough market analysis. Start by developing a bearish thesis on the underlying asset, considering both fundamental and technical factors that support your outlook. Determine your price target and the timeframe in which you expect the bearish move to occur. This analysis will inform your choice of strike prices and expiration date for the spread, ensuring that your strategy aligns with your market expectations. Once you've completed your analysis, select the underlying asset on which you want to implement the bear put spread. This could be an individual stock, an ETF, or even a market index, depending on your outlook and the available options. Choose an expiration date that aligns with your expected timeframe for the bearish move to occur. Remember that options with more time until expiration will be more expensive, but they also give your thesis more time to play out. Balancing the cost of the options with the time needed for your expected move is a crucial consideration in constructing your spread.

Selecting the appropriate strike prices is a crucial decision in constructing your bear put spread. Choose the higher strike price for the put you'll buy and the lower strike price for the put you'll sell. The width between these strikes will determine your maximum profit potential. A wider spread (larger difference between strike prices) will increase both the potential profit and the cost of the spread. Conversely, a narrower spread will limit the potential profit but will be less expensive to implement. Your choice should reflect your specific price target and risk tolerance, as well as your assessment of how far the underlying asset is likely to move within your chosen timeframe.

Determining the right position size is essential for effective risk management. Decide how many spreads to trade based on your risk tolerance and account size. Remember that each spread typically represents 100 shares of the underlying asset. It's generally advisable to limit the risk on any single trade to a small percentage of your overall account value. This approach helps to ensure that no single trade can have a catastrophic impact on your portfolio, even if it results in a maximum loss. When you're ready to place the trade, enter the bear put spread as a single order, specifying both the buy and sell legs simultaneously. This ensures you get filled on both sides of the spread and avoids the risk of only partially completing the strategy. Most modern trading platforms allow you to enter spread orders directly, simplifying the process. However, it's still important to double-check all the details before submitting your order to avoid any costly mistakes.

Before entering the trade, it's crucial to set a clear exit strategy. Determine in advance at what profit level you'll close the position and at what loss level you'll exit to limit your downside. Having predetermined exit points can help you avoid making emotional decisions in the heat of the moment. Some traders set profit targets at a certain percentage of the maximum potential gain, while others may look to technical levels on the chart of the underlying asset. Similarly, having a predetermined stop-loss point can help limit losses if the trade moves against you. Once the trade is executed, it's important to monitor and manage the position as it progresses. Keep track of how the spread's value changes in relation to movements in the underlying asset. Be prepared to adjust or close the trade as market conditions change or as you approach expiration. Some traders actively manage their spreads, potentially closing the position early if a significant portion of the maximum profit has been captured or if their outlook on the underlying asset changes. This active management approach can help maximize profits and minimize risks as market conditions evolve.

When executing a bear put spread, it's crucial to consider the bid-ask spreads of both options. Wide spreads can significantly impact the cost and potential profitability of the strategy. Using limit orders can help ensure you enter the trade at a favorable price. In some cases, traders may choose to leg into the position by entering each side of the spread separately. While this approach can sometimes result in better fills, it carries the risk of adverse price movements between trades and should be attempted only by more experienced traders who are comfortable managing the additional complexity and risk.

It's also important to be aware of the potential for early assignment on the short put, especially if the underlying asset pays dividends. While early assignment is generally rare, it can occur if the short put becomes deeply in-the-money. Understanding the dynamics of early assignment and how to manage such situations is important for any trader using spread strategies. Being prepared for this possibility can help you avoid surprises and manage your positions more effectively. The bear put spread offers traders a way to express a bearish view with defined risk and potentially lower cost compared to outright long puts. However, it's important to remember that this strategy caps your potential profit, which may be a significant drawback in strongly bearish markets. Traders must weigh this limitation against the benefits of reduced cost and defined risk when deciding whether a bear put spread is appropriate for a given situation. In some cases, traders might choose to use multiple spreads or combine the strategy with other bearish positions to increase their potential profit while still maintaining some level of risk control.

As with any options strategy, success with bear put spreads requires thorough understanding, careful planning, and disciplined execution. Traders should practice implementing these spreads in a paper trading account before risking real capital. Additionally, it's valuable to analyze the performance of your spreads over time, learning from both successful and unsuccessful trades to refine your approach. This ongoing process of review and improvement is crucial for developing proficiency with any options strategy. The bear put spread is a versatile and powerful tool in the options trader's arsenal. It provides a way to express a bearish outlook with defined risk and potentially lower cost than simple long put positions. By mastering this strategy, traders can expand their ability to profit from bearish market moves while maintaining better control over their risk exposure. Whether used for speculation, hedging, or as part of a more complex options strategy, bear put spreads offer traders a flexible and potentially effective way to navigate bearish market conditions.

The Iron Condor

The iron condor is a popular options strategy that belongs to the family of neutral strategies, designed to profit from low volatility or range-bound markets. This strategy involves simultaneously holding a bull put spread and a bear call spread on the same underlying asset with the same expiration date. The iron condor is favored by many options traders for its potential to generate income with limited risk, making it an attractive choice for those seeking to profit from time decay and stable market conditions. At its core, an iron condor consists of four options contracts: two calls and two puts. The strategy is created by selling an out-of-the-money put, buying a further out-of-the-money put (creating a bull put spread), selling an out-of-the-money call, and buying a further out-of-the-money call (creating a bear call spread). All four options have the same expiration date but different strike prices. The name "iron condor" comes from the shape of the profit/loss diagram, which resembles a large-bodied bird with wings spread out.

The basic mechanics of an iron condor can be understood by breaking down its components. The bull put spread (selling a put and buying a lower strike put) provides a bullish outlook, profiting if the underlying asset stays above the sold put's strike price. The bear call spread (selling a call and buying a higher strike call) provides a bearish outlook, profiting if the underlying asset stays below the sold call's strike price. When combined, these spreads create a range within which the strategy is profitable. The maximum profit for an iron condor is achieved when the underlying asset's price at expiration is between the two sold options' strike prices. In this scenario, all four options expire worthless, and the trader keeps the entire net credit received when entering the position. The maximum loss is limited and occurs when the underlying asset's price at expiration is below the lower long put strike or above the higher long call strike. The risk is limited to the difference between the strike prices of either spread minus the net credit received.

Iron condors are particularly useful in several scenarios. When you expect the underlying asset to remain relatively stable or trade within a specific range, an iron condor allows you to profit from this lack of significant price movement. This makes it an excellent strategy for markets that are consolidating or experiencing low volatility. Additionally, iron condors can be effective in high implied volatility environments, where option premiums are inflated. By selling options in these conditions, traders can potentially benefit from volatility contraction.

Another scenario where iron condors can be valuable is when you want to generate income in your portfolio without taking a strong directional view on the market. The strategy allows you to collect premium while maintaining a neutral outlook, which can be particularly attractive in uncertain market conditions or when you don't have a strong conviction about market direction. Risk management is a key benefit of the iron condor strategy. By defining both the potential profit and maximum loss at the outset of the trade, traders can precisely control their risk exposure. This defined risk profile makes iron condors suitable for risk-averse traders or those who prefer strategies with clearly understood outcomes. The strategy also allows for adjustments if the underlying asset begins to move outside the profitable range, providing flexibility in managing the position.

Implementing an iron condor involves several key steps, beginning with thorough market analysis. Start by identifying an underlying asset that you expect to remain relatively stable. This could be an individual stock, an ETF, or a market index.

Consider both technical and fundamental factors that support your neutral outlook. Look for assets trading in a clear range or showing signs of low volatility. Additionally, examine the implied volatility of the options on the asset, as higher implied volatility can lead to more attractive premium collection opportunities. Once you've selected your underlying asset, choose an expiration date for your iron condor. The choice of expiration will depend on your outlook and risk tolerance. Shorter-term expirations (30-45 days) are popular among many iron condor traders as they allow for more frequent trading opportunities and faster time decay. However, longer-term expirations can provide larger premiums and more time for adjustments if needed. Consider your trading style and the characteristics of the underlying asset when making this decision.

Selecting the appropriate strike prices is crucial in constructing your iron condor. For the bull put spread component, choose a strike price for the short put that's below the current price of the underlying asset and has a low probability of being in-the-money at expiration. Then select a lower strike price for the long put, which will define your maximum loss on the put side. For the bear call spread component, choose a strike price for the short call that's above the current price of the underlying asset and has a low probability of being in-the-money at expiration. Then select a higher strike price for the long call, which will define your maximum loss on the call side. The width between the strike prices in each spread will determine your maximum potential loss and the amount of margin required to hold the position. Wider spreads increase both the potential profit and the maximum loss. Consider your risk tolerance and account size when deciding on the width of your spreads. Many traders aim for a potential profit that's about one-third of the maximum loss, but this can vary based on market conditions and individual preferences.

Determining the right position size is essential for effective risk management. Decide how many iron condors to trade based on your risk tolerance and account size. Remember that each iron condor typically represents 100 shares of the underlying asset. It's generally advisable to limit the risk on any single trade to a small percentage of your overall account value, often 1-3%. This approach helps ensure that no single trade can have a catastrophic impact on your portfolio, even if it results in a maximum loss. When you're ready to place the trade, enter the iron condor as a single order, specifying all four legs simultaneously. This ensures you get filled on all components of the spread and avoids the risk of only partially completing the strategy. Most modern trading platforms allow you to enter complex orders like iron condors directly, simplifying the process. However, it's still important to double-check all the details before submitting your order to avoid any costly mistakes.

Before entering the trade, it's crucial to set a clear exit strategy. Determine in advance at what profit level you'll close the position and at what loss level you'll exit to limit your downside.

Many iron condor traders aim to close the position when they've captured 50-75% of the maximum potential profit, as the risk-reward ratio becomes less favorable as you approach expiration. Similarly, having a predetermined stop-loss point, such as a specific dollar amount or a certain percentage of the maximum loss, can help limit losses if the underlying asset moves outside your expected range. Once the trade is executed, it's important to monitor and manage the position as it progresses. Keep track of how the iron condor's value changes in relation to movements in the underlying asset. Be prepared to adjust or close the trade as market conditions change or as you approach expiration. Some traders actively manage their iron condors, potentially rolling one side of the spread if the underlying asset moves too close to one of the short strikes. This active management approach can help maintain the desired risk profile and potentially increase the overall profitability of the strategy.

When executing an iron condor, it's crucial to consider the bid-ask spreads of all four options involved. Wide spreads can significantly impact the cost and potential profitability of the strategy. Using limit orders can help ensure you enter the trade at a favorable price. In some cases, traders may choose to leg into the position by entering each spread separately. While this approach can sometimes result in better fills, it carries the risk of adverse price movements between trades and should be attempted only by more experienced traders who are comfortable managing the additional complexity and risk.

It's also important to be aware of potential early assignment risks, especially if the underlying asset pays dividends. While early assignment is generally rare for out-of-the-money options, it can occur if one of the short options becomes in-the-money. Understanding the dynamics of early assignment and how to manage such situations is important for any trader using spread strategies. Being prepared for this possibility can help you avoid surprises and manage your positions more effectively. The iron condor offers traders a way to potentially profit from range-bound markets with defined risk. However, it's important to remember that this strategy has limited profit potential and can face significant losses if the underlying asset makes a large move in either direction. Traders must weigh the high probability of smaller profits against the risk of larger losses when deciding whether an iron condor is appropriate for a given situation. In some cases, traders might choose to use multiple iron condors or combine the strategy with other positions to create a more comprehensive trading approach.

One of the key advantages of the iron condor is its ability to profit from time decay. As options approach expiration, they tend to lose value due to time decay (theta). Since the iron condor involves selling options, this time decay works in the trader's favor. However, this also means that the strategy can be sensitive to changes in implied volatility. A significant increase in implied volatility can negatively impact the position, even if the underlying asset remains within the desired range. Another factor to consider when trading iron condors is the impact of market volatility. While the strategy is designed to profit from low volatility environments, unexpected spikes in volatility can quickly turn a profitable position into a losing one. It's important to stay informed about potential market-moving events and to have a plan for managing your iron condors in case of sudden increases in volatility.

Iron condors can also be adjusted to reflect different market outlooks. For example, if you have a slightly bullish bias, you might place the put spread closer to the current price of the underlying asset and the call spread further away. This creates an unbalanced or "skewed" iron condor that has a higher probability of profiting from small upward movements while still maintaining protection against large moves in either direction. As with any options strategy, success with iron condors requires thorough understanding, careful planning, and disciplined execution. Traders should practice implementing these spreads in a paper trading account before risking real capital. Additionally, it's valuable to analyze the performance of your iron condors over time, learning from both successful and unsuccessful trades to refine your approach. This ongoing process of review and improvement is crucial for developing proficiency with any options strategy.

The iron condor is a versatile and powerful tool in the options trader's arsenal. It provides a way to potentially profit from range-bound markets while maintaining defined risk. By mastering this strategy, traders can expand their ability to generate income in various market conditions, particularly when volatility is low or when they don't have a strong directional bias. Whether used as a standalone strategy or as part of a more complex options approach, iron condors offer traders a flexible and potentially effective way to navigate neutral market conditions. As traders become more comfortable with iron condors, they may explore variations of the strategy, such as broken wing iron condors or iron butterflies. These variations allow for further customization of the risk-reward profile to suit specific market outlooks or risk preferences. The key to success with iron condors, as with all options strategies, lies in thorough preparation, careful risk management, and ongoing education and refinement of your trading approach.

The Straddle

The straddle is a popular options strategy that allows traders to profit from significant price movements in either direction, without needing to predict whether the move will be up or down. This non-directional strategy involves simultaneously buying a call option and a put option with the same strike price and expiration date on the same underlying asset. The straddle is particularly useful when a trader anticipates a large price move but is unsure of the direction, making it a valuable tool for volatile markets or ahead of significant events that could impact an asset's price.

At its core, a long straddle consists of two options contracts: a call and a put. Both options have the same underlying asset, strike price, and expiration date. The trader buys both options, which means they're paying two premiums and taking on the role of the option holder for both contracts. This dual purchase gives the trader the right, but not the obligation, to both buy (via the call) and sell (via the put) the underlying asset at the strike price before or at expiration. The basic mechanics of a straddle can be understood by examining its components. The long call option gives the trader the right to buy the underlying asset at the strike price. As the asset's price increases above the strike price plus the total premium paid, this option becomes profitable. Conversely, the long put option gives the trader the right to sell the underlying asset at the strike price. As the asset's price decreases below the strike price minus the total premium paid, this option becomes profitable. The combination of these two options creates a position that can profit from a move in either direction, as long as the move is large enough to overcome the total cost of the premiums.

The profit potential for a long straddle is theoretically unlimited on the upside (due to the call option) and limited only by the underlying asset reaching zero on the downside (due to the put option). The maximum loss is limited to the total premium paid for both options, which occurs if the underlying asset's price at expiration is exactly at the strike price, causing both options to expire worthless. The break-even points for a straddle are calculated by adding and subtracting the total premium paid from the strike price. Straddles are particularly useful in several scenarios. One of the most common applications is when a trader anticipates a significant market-moving event but is uncertain about the direction of the move. This could be ahead of earnings announcements, regulatory decisions, clinical trial results for pharmaceutical companies, or any other event that could cause a large price swing. By implementing a straddle, the trader can potentially profit regardless of whether the news is positive or negative, as long as the resulting price move is large enough.

Another scenario where straddles can be valuable is during periods of low volatility that are expected to be followed by increased volatility. If a trader believes that an asset has been trading in a tight range but is likely to break out in either direction, a straddle can provide exposure to this anticipated increase in volatility. This makes straddles a popular choice for traders who have a view on volatility rather than on price direction. Straddles can also be used as a hedging tool in certain situations. For example, if a trader has a large position in an underlying asset and wants to protect against potential losses without giving up the possibility of gains, a straddle can provide this two-way protection. While this is generally a more expensive form of hedging compared to simply buying a protective put, it allows the trader to maintain full upside potential.

Implementing a straddle involves several key steps, beginning with thorough market analysis. Start by identifying an underlying asset that you expect to experience a significant price move. This could be an individual stock, an ETF, or a market index. Consider both technical and fundamental factors that support your expectation of increased volatility or a large price move. Look for assets with upcoming events that could cause significant price swings, or those that have been trading in a tight range and may be due for a breakout. Once you've selected your underlying asset, choose an expiration date for your straddle. The choice of expiration will depend on your outlook and the timing of any anticipated events. If you're trading a straddle around a specific event, such as an earnings announcement, you'll typically want to choose an expiration date shortly after the event. For more general volatility plays, longer-term expirations might be appropriate. Keep in mind that longer-term options will be more expensive but will give your thesis more time to play out.

Selecting the appropriate strike price is crucial in constructing your straddle. Typically, straddles are implemented using at-the-money options, meaning the strike price is as close as possible to the current price of the underlying asset. This provides a balanced exposure to moves in either direction. However, some traders might choose to implement a slightly bullish or bearish bias by selecting a strike price slightly above or below the current asset price. Determining the right position size is essential for effective risk management. Decide how many straddles to trade based on your risk tolerance and account size. Remember that each straddle typically represents 100 shares of the underlying asset, and you're buying both a call and a put, so the total cost can be significant. It's generally advisable to limit the risk on any single trade to a small percentage of your overall account value, often 1-3%. This approach helps ensure that no single trade can have a catastrophic impact on your portfolio, even if it results in a maximum loss.

When you're ready to place the trade, enter the straddle as a single order, specifying both the call and put legs simultaneously. This ensures you get filled on both options at the same time, avoiding any risk of market movement between separate orders. Most modern trading platforms allow you to enter straddle orders directly, simplifying the process. However, it's still important to double-check all the details before submitting your order to avoid any costly mistakes.

Before entering the trade, it's crucial to set a clear exit strategy. Determine in advance at what profit level you'll close the position and at what loss level you'll exit to limit your downside. Many straddle traders aim to close the position if they achieve a certain percentage of profit, such as 50% or 100% of the initial investment. Similarly, having a predetermined stop-loss point can help limit losses if the underlying asset fails to make the anticipated move.

Once the trade is executed, it's important to monitor and manage the position actively. Keep track of how the straddle's value changes in relation to movements in the underlying asset and changes in implied volatility. Be prepared to adjust or close the trade as market conditions change or as you approach expiration. Some traders actively manage their straddles, potentially closing one side of the position if the underlying asset makes a significant move in one direction, leaving the other side open for potential further gains. When executing a straddle, it's crucial to consider the impact of implied volatility on the options prices. Straddles are often expensive to implement, particularly when implied volatility is high. However, high implied volatility also suggests that the market expects significant price movements, which is favorable for the straddle strategy. Be aware that a decrease in implied volatility after you enter the position can negatively impact the value of your straddle, even if the underlying asset price moves in your favor.

It's also important to be aware of potential early assignment risks, especially if the underlying asset pays dividends. While early assignment is generally rare for at-the-money options, it can occur if one of the options becomes significantly in-the-money. Understanding the dynamics of early assignment and how to manage such situations is important for any trader using options strategies. The straddle offers traders a way to potentially profit from significant price movements without needing to predict the direction. However, it's important to remember that this strategy can be expensive to implement and requires a large move in the underlying asset to be profitable. Traders must weigh the potential for large profits against the high cost and the risk of losing the entire premium paid if the anticipated move doesn't materialize.

One of the key advantages of the straddle is its ability to profit from increased volatility. As market volatility increases, the value of both the call and put options typically rises, benefiting the straddle position. This makes straddles a popular choice for traders who have a view on future volatility rather than on price direction. However, this also means that the strategy can be negatively impacted by decreases in volatility, even if the underlying asset price remains unchanged. Another factor to consider when trading straddles is the impact of time decay. As options approach expiration, they lose value due to time decay (theta). Since the straddle involves buying options, this time decay works against the trader. This means that even if the underlying asset price remains unchanged, the value of the straddle will decrease over time. This time decay accelerates as expiration approaches, which is why many traders avoid holding long straddles into the final weeks before expiration unless they have a strong conviction about an impending price move.

Straddles can also be adjusted to reflect different market outlooks. For example, if you have a slight directional bias but still want to profit from a large move in either direction, you might implement a strangle instead of a straddle. A strangle involves buying out-of-the-money call and put options, which reduces the cost of the strategy but requires an even larger price move to be profitable. As with any options strategy, success with straddles requires thorough understanding, careful planning, and disciplined execution. Traders should practice implementing these strategies in a paper trading account before risking real capital. Additionally, it's valuable to analyze the performance of your straddles over time, learning from both successful and unsuccessful trades to refine your approach. This ongoing process of review and improvement is crucial for developing proficiency with any options strategy.

The straddle is a versatile and powerful tool in the options trader's arsenal. It provides a way to potentially profit from significant price movements or increases in volatility without needing to predict market direction. By mastering this strategy, traders can expand their ability to navigate uncertain market conditions and capitalize on events that are expected to cause large price swings. Whether used as a standalone strategy or as part of a more complex options approach, straddles offer traders a flexible and potentially effective way to trade volatility and significant market events.

The Strangle

The strangle is a popular options strategy that, like the straddle, allows traders to profit from significant price movements in either direction without needing to predict whether the move will be up or down. However, the strangle differs from the straddle in its structure and risk-reward profile. This non-directional strategy involves simultaneously buying an out-of-the-money call option and an out-of-the-money put option with the same expiration date on the same underlying asset. The strangle is particularly useful when a trader anticipates a large price move but is unsure of the direction and wants a less expensive alternative to the straddle. At its core, a long strangle consists of two options contracts: an out-of-the-money call and an out-of-the-money put. Both options have the same underlying asset and expiration date, but different strike prices. The trader buys both options, which means they're paying two premiums and taking on the role of the option holder for both contracts. This dual purchase gives the trader the right, but not the obligation, to both buy (via the call) and sell (via the put) the underlying asset at their respective strike prices before or at expiration.

The basic mechanics of a strangle can be understood by examining its components. The long call option gives the trader the right to buy the underlying asset at the higher strike price. As the asset's price increases above this strike price plus the total premium paid, this option becomes profitable. Conversely, the long put option gives the trader the right to sell the underlying asset at the lower strike price. As the asset's price decreases below this strike price minus the total premium paid, this option becomes profitable. The combination of these two out-of-the-money options creates a position that can profit from a move in either direction, as long as the move is large enough to overcome the total cost of the premiums. The profit potential for a long strangle is theoretically unlimited on the upside (due to the call option) and limited only by the underlying asset reaching zero on the downside (due to the put option). The maximum loss is limited to the total premium paid for both options, which occurs if the underlying asset's price at expiration is between the two strike prices, causing both options to expire worthless. The break-even points for a strangle are calculated by adding the total premium paid to the call strike price for the upside breakeven, and subtracting the total premium paid from the put strike price for the downside breakeven.

Strangles are particularly useful in several scenarios. One of the most common applications is when a trader anticipates a significant market-moving event but is uncertain about the direction of the move and wants a less expensive alternative to a straddle. This could be ahead of earnings announcements, regulatory decisions, economic data releases, or any other event that could cause a large price swing. By implementing a strangle, the trader can potentially profit regardless of whether the news is positive or negative, as long as the resulting price move is large enough to surpass one of the break-even points. Another scenario where strangles can be valuable is during periods of low volatility that are expected to be followed by increased volatility. If a trader believes that an asset has been trading in a tight range but is likely to break out in either direction, a strangle can provide exposure to this anticipated increase in volatility at a lower cost than a straddle. This makes strangles a popular choice for traders who have a view on volatility rather than on price direction and are willing to accept a larger required price move for profitability in exchange for lower upfront costs.

Strangles can also be used as a hedging tool in certain situations. For example, if a trader has a large position in an underlying asset and wants to protect against potential extreme losses without giving up too much upside potential, a strangle can provide this two-way protection at a lower cost than a straddle. While this is still a more expensive form of hedging compared to simply buying a protective put, it allows the trader to maintain full upside potential beyond the call strike price. Implementing a strangle involves several key steps, beginning with thorough market analysis. Start by identifying an underlying asset that you expect to experience a significant price move. This could be an individual stock, an ETF, or a market index. Consider both technical and fundamental factors that support your expectation of increased volatility or a large price move. Look for assets with upcoming events that could cause significant price swings, or those that have been trading in a tight range and may be due for a breakout.

Once you've selected your underlying asset, choose an expiration date for your strangle. The choice of expiration will depend on your outlook and the timing of any anticipated events. If you're trading a strangle around a specific event, such as an earnings announcement, you'll typically want to choose an expiration date shortly after the event. For more general volatility plays, longer-term expirations might be appropriate. Keep in mind that longer-term options will be more expensive but will give your thesis more time to play out. Selecting the appropriate strike prices is crucial in constructing your strangle. Unlike a straddle, which typically uses at-the-money options, a strangle uses out-of-the-money options. You'll need to choose a call strike price above the current asset price and a put strike price below it. The wider the spread between these strike prices, the less expensive the strangle will be to implement, but the larger the price move required for profitability. Your choice of strike prices should reflect your assessment of the potential magnitude of the price move and your risk tolerance.

Determining the right position size is essential for effective risk management. Decide how many strangles to trade based on your risk tolerance and account size. Remember that each strangle typically represents 100 shares of the underlying asset, and you're buying both a call and a put, so the total cost can be significant, though generally less than a comparable straddle. It's generally advisable to limit the risk on any single trade to a small percentage of your overall account value, often 1-3%. This approach helps ensure that no single trade can have a catastrophic impact on your portfolio, even if it results in a maximum loss. When you're ready to place the trade, enter the strangle as a single order, specifying both the call and put legs simultaneously. This ensures you get filled on both options at the same time, avoiding any risk of market movement between separate orders. Most modern trading platforms allow you to enter strangle orders directly, simplifying the process. However, it's still important to double-check all the details before submitting your order to avoid any costly mistakes.

Before entering the trade, it's crucial to set a clear exit strategy. Determine in advance at what profit level you'll close the position and at what loss level you'll exit to limit your downside. Many strangle traders aim to close the position if they achieve a certain percentage of profit, such as 50% or 100% of the initial investment. Similarly, having a predetermined stop-loss point can help limit losses if the underlying asset fails to make the anticipated move. Once the trade is executed, it's important to monitor and manage the position actively. Keep track of how the strangle's value changes in relation to movements in the underlying asset and changes in implied volatility. Be prepared to adjust or close the trade as market conditions change or as you approach expiration. Some traders actively manage their strangles, potentially closing one side of the position if the underlying asset makes a significant move in one direction, leaving the other side open for potential further gains.

When executing a strangle, it's crucial to consider the impact of implied volatility on the options prices. While strangles are generally less expensive to implement than straddles, they can still be costly, particularly when implied volatility is high. However, high implied volatility also suggests that the market expects significant price movements, which is favorable for the strangle strategy. Be aware that a decrease in implied volatility after you enter the position can negatively impact the value of your strangle, even if the underlying asset price moves in your favor. It's also important to be aware of potential early assignment risks, especially if the underlying asset pays dividends. While early assignment is generally rare for out-of-the-money options, it can occur if one of the options becomes significantly in-the-money. Understanding the dynamics of early assignment and how to manage such situations is important for any trader using options strategies. The strangle offers traders a way to potentially profit from significant price movements without needing to predict the direction, and at a lower cost than a straddle. However, it's important to remember that this strategy requires a larger move in the underlying asset to be profitable compared to a straddle. Traders must weigh the lower cost and potential for large profits against the higher break even points and the risk of losing the entire premium paid if the anticipated move doesn't materialize.

One of the key advantages of the strangle is its ability to profit from increased volatility at a lower cost than a straddle. As market volatility increases, the value of both the call and put options typically rises, benefiting the strangle position. This makes strangles a popular choice for traders who have a view on future volatility rather than on price direction and are willing to accept a higher break even point in exchange for lower upfront costs. However, this also means that the strategy can be negatively impacted by decreases in volatility, even if the underlying asset price remains unchanged.

Another factor to consider when trading strangles is the impact of time decay. As options approach expiration, they lose value due to time decay (theta). Since the strangle involves buying options, this time decay works against the trader. This means that even if the underlying asset price remains unchanged, the value of the strangle will decrease over time. This time decay accelerates as expiration approaches, which is why many traders avoid holding long strangles into the final weeks before expiration unless they have a strong conviction about an impending price move. Strangles can also be adjusted to reflect different market outlooks or risk preferences. For example, if you want to reduce the cost of the strategy even further, you might implement an asymmetric strangle by choosing strike prices that are not equidistant from the current asset price. This could reflect a slight directional bias while still maintaining exposure to moves in either direction.

As with any options strategy, success with strangles requires thorough understanding, careful planning, and disciplined execution. Traders should practice implementing these strategies in a paper trading account before risking real capital. Additionally, it's valuable to analyze the performance of your strangles over time, learning from both successful and unsuccessful trades to refine your approach. This ongoing process of review and improvement is crucial for developing proficiency with any options strategy. The strangle is a versatile and powerful tool in the options trader's arsenal. It provides a way to potentially profit from significant price movements or increases in volatility without needing to predict market direction, and at a lower cost than a straddle. By mastering this strategy, traders can expand their ability to navigate uncertain market conditions and capitalize on events that are expected to cause large price swings, while managing their risk through lower upfront costs. Whether used as a standalone strategy or as part of a more complex options approach, strangles offer traders a flexible and potentially effective way to trade volatility and significant market events at a more attractive cost point than straddles.

Chapter Four

Advanced Strategies for Experienced Traders

"The only limit to our realization of tomorrow is our doubts of today."

- Franklin D. Roosevelt

As traders become more proficient in options trading, they often seek out more sophisticated strategies that offer unique risk-reward profiles and the potential for higher returns. This chapter delves into advanced options strategies that require a deeper understanding of options mechanics and market dynamics. These strategies are typically more complex to implement and manage, but they can provide experienced traders with powerful tools to navigate various market conditions and express nuanced market views.

The Butterfly Spread

The butterfly spread is a neutral options strategy that derives its name from its payoff diagram, which resembles a butterfly with spread wings. This advanced strategy involves simultaneously holding positions in options at three different strike prices. The butterfly spread is popular among experienced traders for its ability to profit from low volatility or a specific price target, while limiting potential losses.

At its core, a butterfly spread consists of four options contracts with the same expiration date but three different strike prices. The most common form is the long butterfly spread, which is created by buying one call (or put) option at a lower strike price, selling two call (or put) options at a middle strike price, and buying one call (or put) option at a higher strike price. The strike prices are typically equidistant from each other, creating a symmetrical structure. The basic mechanics of a butterfly spread can be understood by breaking down its components. The lower and higher strike options (often referred to as the "wings") are bought, while the two middle strike options (the "body") are sold. This configuration results in a net debit position, meaning the trader pays to enter the trade. The maximum profit is achieved when the underlying asset's price at expiration is exactly at the middle strike price, causing the two sold options to expire worthless while one of the bought options expires in-the-money.

The risk-reward profile of a butterfly spread is unique among options strategies. The maximum profit potential occurs at a single point (the middle strike price), and it's limited to the difference between the adjacent strike prices minus the net premium paid. The maximum loss is also limited and is equal to the net premium paid to enter the position. This occurs when the underlying asset's price at expiration is below the lowest strike price or above the highest strike price, causing all options to expire worthless or all to be exercised, resulting in offsetting positions. Butterfly spreads are particularly useful in several scenarios. One of the most common applications is when a trader has a strong opinion about where a stock will not go, rather than where it will go. If you believe an asset will remain relatively stable around a specific price point, a butterfly spread centered on that price can be an effective way to profit from this view. This makes butterfly spreads popular for trading around significant technical levels or known support/resistance areas.

Another scenario where butterfly spreads can be valuable is in low volatility environments. When implied volatility is low, options premiums are generally cheaper, making it less expensive to construct a butterfly spread. If you expect volatility to remain low or decrease further, a butterfly spread can be an effective way to profit from this outlook. Butterfly spreads can also be used as a way to reduce the cost and risk of directional trades. For example, if you're bullish on a stock but want to limit your potential losses, you could implement a call butterfly spread instead of buying a call option outright. This approach sacrifices some of the unlimited upside potential of a long call in exchange for lower cost and defined risk.

Implementing a butterfly spread involves several key steps, beginning with thorough market analysis. Start by identifying an underlying asset that you expect to trade within a specific range or settle near a particular price at expiration. This could be an individual stock, an ETF, or a market index. Consider both technical and fundamental factors that support your outlook. Look for assets with clear support and resistance levels, or those that have been trading in a tight range and are expected to continue doing so. Once you've selected your underlying asset, choose an expiration date for your butterfly spread. The choice of expiration will depend on your outlook and risk tolerance. Shorter-term expirations (30-45 days) are popular among many butterfly traders as they allow for more frequent trading opportunities and faster time decay. However, longer-term expirations can provide more time for your thesis to play out, albeit at a higher cost. Consider your trading style and the characteristics of the underlying asset when making this decision.

Selecting the appropriate strike prices is crucial in constructing your butterfly spread. For a traditional symmetrical butterfly, you'll need to choose three strike prices: a lower strike, a middle strike, and a higher strike. The middle strike should be at or near your target price for the underlying asset at expiration. The lower and higher strikes should be equidistant from the middle strike. The width between strikes will affect both the cost of the spread and its potential profit. Wider spreads are more expensive but offer larger potential profits, while narrower spreads are cheaper but have smaller profit potential. Determining the right position size is essential for effective risk management. Decide how many butterfly spreads to trade based on your risk tolerance and account size. Remember that each butterfly spread typically involves four options contracts, representing a total of 400 shares of the underlying asset. It's generally advisable to limit the risk on any single trade to a small percentage of your overall account value, often 1-3%. This approach helps ensure that no single trade can have a catastrophic impact on your portfolio, even if it results in a maximum loss.

When you're ready to place the trade, enter the butterfly spread as a single order, specifying all four legs simultaneously. This ensures you get filled on all components of the spread and avoids the risk of only partially completing the strategy. Most modern trading platforms allow you to enter complex orders like butterfly spreads directly, simplifying the process. However, it's still important to double-check all the details before submitting your order to avoid any costly mistakes. Before entering the trade, it's crucial to set a clear exit strategy. Determine in advance at what profit level you'll close the position and at what loss level you'll exit to limit your downside. Many butterfly traders aim to close the position when they've captured 50-75% of the maximum potential profit, as the risk-reward ratio becomes less favorable as you approach expiration. Similarly, having a predetermined stop-loss point, such as a specific dollar amount or a certain percentage of the maximum loss, can help limit losses if the underlying asset moves outside your expected range.

Once the trade is executed, it's important to monitor and manage the position as it progresses. Keep track of how the butterfly spread's value changes in relation to movements in the underlying asset and changes in implied volatility. Be prepared to adjust or close the trade as market conditions change or as you approach expiration. Some traders actively manage their butterfly spreads, potentially adjusting the position if the underlying asset moves away from the center strike. This active management approach can help maintain the desired risk profile and potentially increase the overall profitability of the strategy. When executing a butterfly spread, it's crucial to consider the impact of implied volatility on the options prices. Butterfly spreads are generally vega negative, meaning they benefit from decreases in implied volatility. However, the impact of volatility changes can be complex, affecting the different legs of the spread in different ways. Be aware that changes in implied volatility can significantly impact the value of your spread, even if the underlying asset price remains unchanged.

It's also important to be aware of potential early assignment risks, especially if the underlying asset pays dividends. While early assignment is generally rare for out-of-the-money options, it can occur if one of the short options becomes in-the-money. Understanding the dynamics of early assignment and how to manage such situations is important for any trader using spread strategies. The butterfly spread offers traders a way to potentially profit from a specific price target or range with defined risk. However, it's important to remember that this strategy has limited profit potential and requires precise timing and price movement to achieve maximum profitability. Traders must weigh the high probability of smaller profits against the lower probability of achieving maximum profit when deciding whether a butterfly spread is appropriate for a given situation.

One of the key advantages of the butterfly spread is its ability to profit from time decay. As options approach expiration, they tend to lose value due to time decay (theta). Since the butterfly spread involves selling options at the middle strike, this time decay can work in the trader's favor, especially as expiration approaches. However, this also means that the strategy can be sensitive to changes in implied volatility and underlying asset price movements, particularly in the early stages of the trade. Another factor to consider when trading butterfly spreads is the impact of transaction costs. Because the strategy involves four separate options contracts, commissions and fees can significantly affect the overall profitability of the trade. It's important to factor these costs into your analysis when determining whether a particular butterfly spread offers an attractive risk-reward profile.

As with any advanced options strategy, success with butterfly spreads requires thorough understanding, careful planning, and disciplined execution. Traders should practice implementing these spreads in a paper trading account before risking real capital. Additionally, it's valuable to analyze the performance of your butterfly spreads over time, learning from both successful and unsuccessful trades to refine your approach. This ongoing process of review and improvement is crucial for developing proficiency with any options strategy. The butterfly spread is a sophisticated tool in the experienced options trader's arsenal. It provides a way to potentially profit from specific price targets or ranges while maintaining defined risk. By mastering this strategy, traders can expand their ability to express nuanced market views and capitalize on low volatility environments. Whether used as a standalone strategy or as part of a more complex options approach, butterfly spreads offer traders a flexible and potentially effective way to navigate specific market conditions with precision.

The Calendar Spread

The calendar spread, also known as a time spread or horizontal spread, is an advanced options strategy that involves simultaneously buying and selling options of the same type (calls or puts) and strike price, but with different expiration dates. This strategy allows traders to capitalize on the different rates of time decay between near-term and longer-term options, as well as potential changes in implied volatility. Calendar spreads are popular among experienced traders for their ability to profit from sideways markets and their unique risk-reward characteristics.

At its core, a calendar spread consists of two options contracts: one short-term option that is sold, and one longer-term option that is bought. Both options have the same underlying asset and strike price, but different expiration dates. The most common form is the long calendar spread, where the trader sells the near-term option and buys the longer-term option. This configuration typically results in a net debit position, meaning the trader pays to enter the trade. The basic mechanics of a calendar spread can be understood by examining its components. The short-term option that is sold generates immediate income and has a higher rate of time decay. This means its value erodes more quickly as expiration approaches. The longer-term option that is bought decays more slowly, preserving more of its value over time. The goal is for the short-term option to lose value more rapidly than the long-term option, ideally expiring worthless while the longer-term option retains value.

The risk-reward profile of a calendar spread is more complex than many other options strategies. The maximum profit potential is theoretically unlimited but practically limited, occurring when the underlying asset's price at the near-term expiration is exactly at the strike price of both options. At this point, the short-term option expires worthless, while the longer-term option retains its full value. The maximum loss is limited to the net premium paid to enter the position, which occurs if the underlying asset's price moves significantly away from the strike price in either direction before the near-term expiration. Calendar spreads are particularly useful in several scenarios. One of the most common applications is when a trader expects an asset to remain relatively stable in the short term but potentially become more volatile in the longer term. By selling the short-term option to capitalize on rapid time decay and buying the longer-term option to benefit from potential future price movements or volatility increases, the trader can potentially profit from both the near-term stability and longer-term uncertainty. Another scenario where calendar spreads can be valuable is in low volatility environments. When implied volatility is low, options premiums are generally cheaper, making it less expensive to construct a calendar spread. If you expect volatility to remain low in the short term but potentially increase in the future, a calendar spread can be an effective way to position for this outlook.

Calendar spreads can also be used as a way to reduce the cost of longer-term options positions. By selling short-term options against a longer-term option holding, traders can generate income to offset some of the cost of the longer-term option. This approach can be particularly useful when implementing longer-term directional views or when looking to maintain exposure to potential large moves while reducing carrying costs. Implementing a calendar spread involves several key steps, beginning with thorough market analysis. Start by identifying an underlying asset that you expect to trade within a specific range in the short term but potentially become more volatile in the longer term. This could be an individual stock, an ETF, or a market index. Consider both technical and fundamental factors that support your outlook. Look for assets with clear support and resistance levels in the near term, or those that have upcoming events that could drive volatility in the future.

Once you've selected your underlying asset, choose the expiration dates for your calendar spread. The choice of expirations will depend on your outlook and risk tolerance. Typically, the near-term option might have 30-45 days until expiration, while the longer-term option might be 60-90 days out or more. The wider the gap between expirations, the more expensive the spread will be to implement, but it will also provide more time for your thesis to play out. Selecting the appropriate strike price is crucial in constructing your calendar spread. Typically, calendar spreads are implemented using at-the-money options, meaning the strike price is close to the current price of the underlying asset. This provides the highest probability of the short-term option expiring worthless if the asset remains stable. However, some traders might choose to implement slightly bullish or bearish calendar spreads by selecting a strike price slightly above or below the current asset price.

Determining the right position size is essential for effective risk management. Decide how many calendar spreads to trade based on your risk tolerance and account size. Remember that each calendar spread typically involves two options contracts, representing a total of 200 shares of the underlying asset. It's generally advisable to limit the risk on any single trade to a small percentage of your overall account value, often 1-3%. This approach helps ensure that no single trade can have a catastrophic impact on your portfolio, even if it results in a maximum loss. When you're ready to place the trade, enter the calendar spread as a single order, specifying both legs simultaneously. This ensures you get filled on both components of the spread and avoids the risk of only partially completing the strategy. Most modern trading platforms allow you to enter calendar spread orders directly, simplifying the process.

However, it's still important to double-check all the details before submitting your order to avoid any costly mistakes.

Before entering the trade, it's crucial to set a clear exit strategy. Determine in advance at what profit level you'll close the position and at what loss level you'll exit to limit your downside. Many calendar spread traders aim to close the position when they've captured a certain percentage of the maximum potential profit, or when the short-term option approaches expiration. Having a predetermined stop-loss point can help limit losses if the underlying asset moves significantly away from the strike price. Once the trade is executed, it's important to monitor and manage the position actively. Keep track of how the calendar spread's value changes in relation to movements in the underlying asset and changes in implied volatility. Be prepared to adjust or close the trade as market conditions change or as you approach the near-term expiration. Some traders actively manage their calendar spreads, potentially rolling the short-term option to a new expiration date if the initial outlook remains valid.

When executing a calendar spread, it's crucial to consider the impact of implied volatility on the options prices. Calendar spreads are generally vega positive, meaning they benefit from increases in implied volatility. However, the impact of volatility changes can be complex, potentially affecting the short-term and long-term options differently. Be aware that changes in implied volatility can significantly impact the value of your spread, even if the underlying asset price remains unchanged.

It's also important to be aware of potential early assignment risks, especially if the underlying asset pays dividends. While early assignment is generally rare for at-the-money options, it can occur if the underlying asset moves significantly. Understanding the dynamics of early assignment and how to manage such situations is important for any trader using spread strategies.

The calendar spread offers traders a way to potentially profit from the different rates of time decay between options with different expiration dates, as well as from anticipated changes in volatility. However, it's important to remember that this strategy can be complex to manage and may require precise timing to achieve maximum profitability. Traders must carefully consider the potential risks and rewards, including the impact of volatility changes and underlying asset price movements, when deciding whether a calendar spread is appropriate for a given situation. One of the key advantages of the calendar spread is its ability to profit from time decay while maintaining exposure to potential future price movements. As the short-term option approaches expiration, it typically loses value more rapidly than the longer-term option, potentially creating profitable opportunities. However, this also means that the strategy can be sensitive to changes in implied volatility and underlying asset price movements, particularly as the near-term expiration approaches.

Another factor to consider when trading calendar spreads is the impact of dividends. If the underlying asset pays a dividend between the two expiration dates, this can affect the pricing and behavior of the options. It's important to be aware of any upcoming dividends and factor them into your analysis when constructing and managing calendar spreads. As with any advanced options strategy, success with calendar spreads requires thorough understanding, careful planning, and disciplined execution. Traders should practice implementing these spreads in a paper trading account before risking real capital. Additionally, it's valuable to analyze the performance of your calendar spreads over time, learning from both successful and unsuccessful trades to refine your approach. This ongoing process of review and improvement is crucial for developing proficiency with this sophisticated options strategy.

The calendar spread represents a sophisticated approach for options traders seeking to capitalize on time decay and volatility dynamics. This strategy enables investors to express nuanced market views and potentially profit from sideways price action. By mastering calendar spreads, traders can enhance their ability to navigate complex market conditions and exploit the term structure of option prices. Whether employed independently or as part of a broader options strategy, calendar spreads provide a versatile method for experienced traders to fine-tune their market exposure and potentially generate returns in various market environments.

The Diagonal Spread

The diagonal spread is an advanced options strategy that combines elements of both vertical and calendar spreads. This versatile approach involves simultaneously buying and selling options of the same type (calls or puts) but with different strike prices and expiration dates. Diagonal spreads offer traders a unique way to capitalize on both directional moves and time decay, making them a valuable tool for experienced options traders seeking to fine-tune their market exposure. At its core, a diagonal spread consists of two options contracts: one longer-term option that is bought, and one shorter-term option that is sold. Unlike calendar spreads, where the strike prices are the same, diagonal spreads use different strike prices for each leg. This configuration typically results in a net debit position, though in some cases it can be structured as a net credit trade.

The basic mechanics of a diagonal spread can be understood by examining its components. The longer-term option that is bought provides the foundation of the position, offering exposure to potential price movements over an extended period. The shorter-term option that is sold generates immediate income and benefits from more rapid time decay. The goal is to profit from a combination of favorable price movement, time decay of the short option, and potentially beneficial changes in implied volatility. The risk-reward profile of a diagonal spread is more complex than many other options strategies. The maximum profit and loss potentials can vary significantly depending on the specific strike prices and expiration dates chosen. Generally, the maximum loss is limited to the net premium paid (for a debit spread), while the maximum profit can be substantial but is typically not unlimited. The strategy's profitability is influenced by changes in the underlying asset's price, time decay, and shifts in implied volatility.

Diagonal spreads are particularly useful in several scenarios. One common application is when a trader has a moderately bullish or bearish outlook over the longer term but expects limited movement in the near term. By selling a shorter-term option, the trader can generate income and benefit from time decay, while the longer-term option provides exposure to the anticipated directional move. Another scenario where diagonal spreads can be valuable is when a trader wants to reduce the cost of a longer-term options position. By selling a shorter-term option against a longer-term holding, traders can offset some of the initial cost and potentially improve the overall risk-reward profile of their position. Diagonal spreads can also be effective in volatile markets or when significant events are expected. The different expiration dates allow traders to potentially benefit from changes in implied volatility across different time frames, while the different strike prices provide a degree of directional exposure.

Implementing a diagonal spread involves several key steps, beginning with thorough market analysis. Start by identifying an underlying asset that aligns with your market outlook. Consider both short-term and longer-term factors that could influence the asset's price movement and volatility. Assess technical indicators, fundamental data, and any upcoming events that could impact your chosen underlying asset. Once you've selected your underlying asset, choose the expiration dates for your diagonal spread. The choice of expirations will depend on your outlook and risk tolerance. Typically, the near-term option might have 30-45 days until expiration, while the longer-term option could be several months out. The wider the gap between expirations, the more the spread will behave like a diagonal strategy rather than a vertical spread.

Selecting the appropriate strike prices is crucial in constructing your diagonal spread. For a bullish diagonal spread using calls, you might buy a longer-term in-the-money call and sell a shorter-term out-of-the-money call. For a bearish diagonal spread using puts, you could buy a longer-term in-the-money put and sell a shorter-term out-of-the-money put. The choice of strike prices will significantly impact the strategy's risk-reward profile and its sensitivity to changes in the underlying asset's price. Determining the right position size is essential for effective risk management. Decide how many diagonal spreads to trade based on your risk tolerance and account size. Remember that each spread involves two options contracts, representing a total of 200 shares of the underlying asset. It's generally advisable to limit the risk on any single trade to a small percentage of your overall account value, often 1-3%. When you're ready to place the trade, enter the diagonal spread as a single order, specifying both legs simultaneously. This ensures you get filled on both components of the spread and avoids the risk of only partially completing the strategy. Most modern trading platforms allow you to enter complex spread orders directly, simplifying the process.

Before entering the trade, it's crucial to set a clear exit strategy. Determine in advance at what profit level you'll close the position and at what loss level you'll exit to limit your downside. Many diagonal spread traders aim to close the position when they've captured a certain percentage of the maximum potential profit, or when the short-term option approaches expiration. Having a predetermined stop-loss point can help limit losses if the trade moves against you. Once the trade is executed, it's important to monitor and manage the position actively. Keep track of how the diagonal spread's value changes in relation to movements in the underlying asset, changes in implied volatility, and the passage of time. Be prepared to adjust or close the trade as market conditions change or as you approach the near-term expiration. Some traders actively manage their diagonal spreads, potentially rolling the short-term option to a new expiration date or adjusting strike prices as needed.

When executing a diagonal spread, it's crucial to consider the impact of implied volatility on the options prices. Diagonal spreads can be sensitive to changes in implied volatility, and the impact may differ for the short-term and long-term options. Be aware that changes in implied volatility can significantly affect the value of your spread, even if the underlying asset price remains unchanged. It's also important to be aware of potential early assignment risks, especially if the underlying asset pays dividends. While early assignment is generally rare for out-of-the-money options, it can occur if the short option becomes in-the-money. Understanding the dynamics of early assignment and how to manage such situations is important for any trader using spread strategies.

The diagonal spread offers traders a way to potentially profit from a combination of price movement, time decay, and volatility changes. However, it's important to remember that this strategy can be complex to manage and may require careful monitoring and adjustment. Traders must carefully consider the potential risks and rewards, including the impact of volatility changes and underlying asset price movements, when deciding whether a diagonal spread is appropriate for a given situation. One of the key advantages of the diagonal spread is its flexibility. By adjusting the strike prices and expiration dates, traders can create a wide range of risk-reward profiles to suit their specific market outlook and risk tolerance. This adaptability makes diagonal spreads a valuable addition to an experienced trader's strategic toolkit.

As with any advanced options strategy, success with diagonal spreads requires thorough understanding, careful planning, and disciplined execution. Traders should practice implementing these spreads in a paper trading account before risking real capital. Additionally, it's valuable to analyze the performance of your diagonal spreads over time, learning from both successful and unsuccessful trades to refine your approach. The diagonal spread represents a sophisticated strategy for options traders looking to capitalize on multiple market factors simultaneously. By combining elements of vertical and calendar spreads, this approach enables traders to craft positions that align closely with their market outlook and risk preferences. While challenging to master, diagonal spreads offer experienced traders a powerful means to navigate complex market conditions and potentially generate returns in various scenarios.

The Ratio Spread

The ratio spread is an advanced options strategy that involves buying and selling options of the same type (calls or puts) and expiration date, but in unequal quantities and at different strike prices. This strategy allows traders to potentially profit from specific price movements while partially financing the trade through the sale of multiple options. Ratio spreads offer a unique risk-reward profile that can be tailored to suit various market outlooks and risk tolerances. At its core, a ratio spread consists of buying one or more options at one strike price and selling a larger number of options at a different strike price. The most common ratio is 1:2, where a trader buys one option and sells two, but other ratios such as 1:3 or 2:3 can also be used. The options all have the same expiration date and are typically all calls or all puts. Depending on the structure, a ratio spread can be implemented for a net debit, net credit, or even at no cost.

The basic mechanics of a ratio spread can be understood by examining its components. The long option(s) provide(s) the primary directional exposure and define(s) the maximum loss of the position. The short options, which are sold in greater quantity, help to finance the long option(s) and can potentially generate additional profit if the underlying asset moves favorably. However, these short options also introduce unlimited or significant risk if the underlying asset moves too far in the direction of the short options. The risk-reward profile of a ratio spread is more complex than many other options strategies. The maximum profit typically occurs when the underlying asset's price at expiration is at or near the strike price of the short options. At this point, the long option has some intrinsic value, while the short options expire worthless. The maximum loss can be limited on one side (for a call ratio spread) or potentially unlimited (for a put ratio spread), depending on the direction of the underlying asset's movement.

Ratio spreads are particularly useful in several scenarios. One common application is when a trader expects a moderate move in the underlying asset but believes that a large move is unlikely. The ratio spread allows the trader to profit from the expected moderate move while potentially benefiting from time decay and a decrease in implied volatility. Another scenario where ratio spreads can be valuable is when a trader wants to reduce the cost of a directional options position. By selling multiple options against a long option, traders can significantly reduce their initial outlay or even receive a net credit, while still maintaining exposure to potential price movements.

Ratio spreads can also be effective when a trader has a specific price target in mind for the underlying asset. By carefully selecting the strike prices and ratio, traders can create a position that maximizes profit potential at their target price while limiting risk elsewhere. Implementing a ratio spread involves several key steps, beginning with thorough market analysis. Start by identifying an underlying asset that aligns with your market outlook. Consider factors such as recent price trends, support and resistance levels, upcoming events that could impact the asset, and current volatility levels. Your analysis should support a view on both the direction and magnitude of potential price movements.

Once you've selected your underlying asset, choose the expiration date for your ratio spread. The choice of expiration will depend on your outlook and risk tolerance. Shorter-term expirations (30-45 days) are common for ratio spreads, as they allow traders to benefit from more rapid time decay. However, longer-term expirations can be used if you expect the underlying asset to take more time to reach your target price. Selecting the appropriate strike prices is crucial in constructing your ratio spread. For a call ratio spread, you might buy a lower strike call and sell multiple higher strike calls. For a put ratio spread, you would buy a higher strike put and sell multiple lower strike puts. The choice of strike prices will significantly impact the strategy's risk-reward profile, including the maximum profit potential, breakeven points, and risk exposure.

Determining the right position size and ratio is essential for effective risk management. Decide how many spreads to trade and what ratio to use based on your risk tolerance and account size. Remember that each option contract typically represents 100 shares of the underlying asset. It's generally advisable to limit the risk on any single trade to a small percentage of your overall account value, often 1-3%. Be particularly cautious with ratio spreads, as they can expose you to significant or unlimited risk if the underlying asset moves sharply against your position. When you're ready to place the trade, enter the ratio spread as a single order, specifying all legs simultaneously. This ensures you get filled on all components of the spread and avoids the risk of only partially completing the strategy. Most modern trading platforms allow you to enter complex spread orders directly, simplifying the process.

Before entering the trade, it's crucial to set a clear exit strategy. Determine in advance at what profit level you'll close the position and at what loss level you'll exit to limit your downside. Many ratio spread traders aim to close the position when they've captured a certain percentage of the maximum potential profit, or when the underlying asset approaches their target price. Having predetermined exit points is particularly important for ratio spreads due to their potentially significant risk exposure. Once the trade is executed, it's important to monitor and manage the position actively. Keep track of how the ratio spread's value changes in relation to movements in the underlying asset, changes in implied volatility, and the passage of time. Be prepared to adjust or close the trade as market conditions change or as you approach expiration. Some traders actively manage their ratio spreads, potentially adjusting the position if the underlying asset moves significantly or if market conditions shift.

When executing a ratio spread, it's crucial to consider the impact of implied volatility on the options prices. Ratio spreads can be sensitive to changes in implied volatility, and the impact may differ for the long and short options. Be aware that changes in implied volatility can significantly affect the value of your spread, even if the underlying asset price remains unchanged. It's also important to be aware of potential early assignment risks, especially if the underlying asset pays dividends. While early assignment is generally rare for out-of-the-money options, it can occur if the short options become in-the-money. Understanding the dynamics of early assignment and how to manage such situations is important for any trader using spread strategies, particularly those with undefined risk like ratio spreads.

The ratio spread offers traders a way to potentially profit from specific price movements while partially financing the trade through the sale of multiple options. However, it's important to remember that this strategy can expose traders to significant or unlimited risk if the underlying asset moves sharply in the direction of the short options. Traders must carefully consider the potential risks and rewards, including the impact of large price movements and volatility changes, when deciding whether a ratio spread is appropriate for a given situation. One of the key advantages of the ratio spread is its flexibility in terms of cost and risk-reward profile. By adjusting the strike prices, expiration date, and ratio, traders can create a wide range of positions to suit their specific market outlook and risk tolerance. This adaptability makes ratio spreads a valuable tool for experienced traders looking to fine-tune their options strategies.

As with any advanced options strategy, success with ratio spreads requires thorough understanding, careful planning, and disciplined execution. Traders should practice implementing these spreads in a paper trading account before risking real capital. Additionally, it's valuable to analyze the performance of your ratio spreads over time, learning from both successful and unsuccessful trades to refine your approach. The ratio spread represents a sophisticated strategy for options traders seeking to capitalize on specific price movements while managing costs. By combining long and short options positions in unequal quantities, this approach enables traders to create customized risk-reward profiles that align closely with their market expectations. While potentially rewarding, ratio spreads demand careful risk management and ongoing attention, making them best suited for experienced traders comfortable with complex options positions.

The Box Spread

The box spread is a complex options strategy that involves simultaneously entering into a bull call spread and a bear put spread with the same expiration dates and strike prices. This advanced technique is named for the shape of its profit/loss diagram, which resembles a box. The box spread is primarily used for arbitrage opportunities or as a financing tool, making it a strategy typically employed by institutional traders or highly experienced individual investors.

At its core, a box spread consists of four options contracts: two calls and two puts. Specifically, it involves buying a call option at one strike price and selling a call at a higher strike price (creating a bull call spread), while simultaneously buying a put option at the higher strike price and selling a put at the lower strike price (creating a bear put spread). All four options have the same expiration date. This configuration results in a position that, in theory, should have a fixed value at expiration regardless of the underlying asset's price. The basic mechanics of a box spread can be understood by examining its components. The bull call spread provides upside exposure, while the bear put spread provides downside exposure. When combined, these spreads create a "box" that encompasses all possible prices of the underlying asset at expiration. In a perfectly efficient market, the cost to enter the box spread should equal its guaranteed payout at expiration, minus the effect of interest rates.

The risk-reward profile of a box spread is unique among options strategies. In theory, the strategy should have no risk and no

133

potential for profit, as the value at expiration is known and fixed. However, in practice, inefficiencies in options pricing can create opportunities for arbitrage or allow the box spread to be used as a financing tool. The maximum value of the box at expiration is always equal to the difference between the two strike prices, multiplied by the number of contracts. Box spreads are particularly useful in several specific scenarios. One common application is arbitrage. If the cost to enter the box spread is significantly different from its guaranteed payout at expiration (accounting for interest rates), traders can potentially profit from this mispricing. However, such opportunities are rare and typically close quickly in liquid markets.

Another scenario where box spreads can be valuable is as a financing tool. By constructing a box spread, traders can effectively borrow or lend money at implied interest rates that may be more favorable than those available through traditional means. This use of box spreads is primarily employed by institutional investors and requires careful consideration of transaction costs and margin requirements. Box spreads can also be used for tax purposes in some jurisdictions, allowing traders to potentially convert short-term gains into long-term gains or to defer taxes. However, this application is complex and should only be considered with the guidance of a qualified tax professional. Implementing a box spread involves several key steps, beginning with thorough market analysis. Start by identifying potential inefficiencies in options pricing across different strike prices and expirations. This typically requires sophisticated analytical tools and access to real-time market data. Consider factors such as bid-ask spreads, liquidity, and potential execution costs.

Once you've identified a potential opportunity, choose the expiration date for your box spread. The choice of expiration will depend on your specific objectives, whether for arbitrage or financing purposes. Longer-term expirations may offer larger potential mispricings but also come with increased risks and margin requirements. Selecting the appropriate strike prices is crucial in constructing your box spread. You'll need to choose two strike prices that define the "box." The width of the box (the difference between the strike prices) will determine the guaranteed payout at expiration. Consider the liquidity of options at different strike prices, as well as any potential mispricings that could create an arbitrage opportunity.

Determining the right position size is essential for effective risk management. Decide how many box spreads to trade based on your risk tolerance, account size, and the specific opportunity you've identified. Remember that each box spread involves four options contracts, representing a total of 400 shares of the underlying asset. Be particularly cautious with position sizing for box spreads, as they can require significant margin and may be subject to early assignment risks. When you're ready to place the trade, enter the box spread as a single order, specifying all four legs simultaneously. This ensures you get filled on all components of the spread and avoids the risk of only partially completing the strategy. Most advanced trading platforms allow you to enter complex spread orders like box spreads directly, but you may need to use a specific options-focused broker to access this functionality.

Before entering the trade, it's crucial to thoroughly analyze the potential risks and rewards. Calculate the expected payoff at expiration and compare it to the cost of entering the position, taking into account all transaction costs, potential interest rate effects, and margin requirements. For arbitrage opportunities, ensure that the potential profit justifies the risks and capital commitment. Once the trade is executed, it's important to monitor the position closely. While box spreads theoretically have a fixed value at expiration, they can be subject to significant value fluctuations before expiration due to changes in implied volatility and interest rates. Be prepared to adjust or close the trade if market conditions change or if early assignment becomes a risk.

When executing a box spread, it's crucial to consider the impact of transaction costs, including commissions and bid-ask spreads. These costs can quickly erode or eliminate any potential arbitrage profits. Additionally, be aware of the margin requirements for box spreads, which can be substantial and may vary between brokers.

It's also important to be aware of potential early assignment risks, especially for American-style options. Early assignment of any leg of the box spread can disrupt the strategy and potentially lead to significant losses. Understanding the dynamics of early assignment and how to manage such situations is critical for traders using box spreads.

The box spread offers sophisticated traders a way to potentially capitalize on options mispricing or access unique financing arrangements. However, it's important to remember that this strategy is complex and carries significant risks, including potential losses due to early assignment or unexpected changes in margin requirements. Traders must carefully consider these risks and have a thorough understanding of options mechanics before implementing box spreads. One of the key challenges with box spreads is execution. Due to the strategy's complexity and the tight profit margins often involved, it can be difficult to execute all four legs of the spread at favorable prices. This is particularly true in less liquid options markets or for larger position sizes.

As with any advanced options strategy, success with box spreads requires extensive knowledge, sophisticated analytical tools, and careful risk management. Traders should thoroughly test their approach using simulated trading before committing real capital. Additionally, it's crucial to stay informed about any regulatory changes or broker policies that could affect the viability of box spread strategies. The box spread represents one of the most complex and specialized strategies in the options trading toolkit. While it offers unique opportunities for arbitrage and financing, it demands a level of expertise and risk management capability beyond that required for most other options strategies. For the small subset of traders with the necessary skills and resources, box spreads can provide a powerful tool for exploiting market inefficiencies or optimizing capital utilization. However, for the vast majority of traders, simpler and more straightforward options strategies are likely to be more appropriate and manageable.

Chapter Five

Strategies for Bullish Markets

"Bull markets are born on pessimism, grow on skepticism, mature on optimism, and die on euphoria."
– John Templeton

In the ever-changing landscape of financial markets, periods of bullish sentiment present unique opportunities for options traders. This chapter explores a range of strategies specifically designed to capitalize on upward market movements. Whether you're looking to profit from a strong uptrend, hedge a long stock position, or generate income in a rising market, the strategies outlined here provide a versatile toolkit for navigating bullish conditions. From straightforward long calls to more complex spread strategies, we'll examine how each approach can be tailored to suit different risk tolerances and market outlooks. As we delve into these bullish strategies, remember that successful options trading requires not just a directional view, but also a nuanced understanding of volatility, time decay, and risk management.

Bull Call Spread

The bull call spread is a popular options strategy that allows traders to benefit from an anticipated rise in the price of the underlying asset while limiting both potential profit and risk. This vertical spread strategy involves simultaneously buying a call option at one strike price and selling another call option at a higher strike price, with both options having the same expiration date. The bull call spread is an excellent choice for traders who have a moderately bullish outlook and want to reduce the cost and risk associated with simply buying call options outright. At its core, a bull call spread consists of two call options: one purchased and one sold. The trader buys a call option with a lower strike price and simultaneously sells a call option with a higher strike price. Both options have the same underlying asset and expiration date. The net cost of this position (the debit) is the difference between the premium paid for the long call and the premium received for the short call. This structure allows traders to reduce the cost of taking a bullish position compared to buying a call option outright, as the premium received from selling the higher strike call partially offsets the cost of the lower strike call purchased.

The mechanics of a bull call spread can be understood by examining its components. The long call with the lower strike price provides the primary bullish exposure. As the stock price increases above this strike price, this option gains intrinsic value. The short call with the higher strike price caps the potential profit but reduces the cost of the strategy. The interplay between these two options creates a defined risk-reward profile that many traders find attractive, especially in markets where they expect moderate upside but want to limit their potential losses. Bull call spreads are particularly useful in several scenarios. When you have a moderately bullish outlook, expecting the underlying asset to rise but unsure about significant upside potential, a bull call spread allows you to profit from a moderate increase while limiting your risk. This can be especially valuable in markets where you anticipate steady growth rather than explosive moves. Additionally, in high volatility environments where options premiums are expensive, bull call spreads can provide a more cost-effective way to implement a bullish view compared to buying calls outright.

Another scenario where bull call spreads can be valuable is when you want to reduce the cost and risk of a directional trade. If you're bullish on a stock but want to limit your potential losses, a bull call spread offers a way to express that view with defined risk. This can be particularly appealing for traders who want to maintain strict control over their risk exposure or who are working with smaller accounts where large losses could be particularly detrimental. Implementing a bull call spread involves several key steps, beginning with thorough market analysis. Start by identifying an underlying asset that you expect to appreciate in value. Consider both technical and fundamental factors that support your bullish outlook. Look for assets with clear upward trends, strong fundamentals, or catalysts that could drive price appreciation.

Once you've selected your underlying asset, choose an expiration date for your bull call spread. The choice of expiration will depend on your outlook and risk tolerance. Shorter-term expirations (30-45 days) are popular among many traders as they allow for more frequent trading opportunities and faster time decay of the short call. However, longer-term expirations can provide more time for your bullish thesis to play out, albeit at a higher cost. Selecting the appropriate strike prices is crucial in constructing your bull call spread. Choose a lower strike price for the call you'll buy and a higher strike price for the call you'll sell. The width between these strikes will determine your maximum profit potential and the cost of the spread. A wider spread increases both the potential profit and the cost, while a narrower spread limits the potential profit but is less expensive to implement. Your choice should reflect your specific price target and risk tolerance.

When you're ready to place the trade, enter the bull call spread as a single order, specifying both the buy and sell legs simultaneously. This ensures you get filled on both sides of the spread and avoids the risk of only partially completing the strategy. Most modern trading platforms allow you to enter spread orders directly, simplifying the process. Before entering the trade, it's crucial to set a clear exit strategy. Determine in advance at what profit level you'll close the position and at what loss level you'll exit to limit your downside. Many traders aim to close the position when they've captured 50-75% of the maximum potential profit, as the risk-reward ratio becomes less favorable as you approach expiration.

Once the trade is executed, monitor the position closely. Keep track of how the spread's value changes in relation to movements in the underlying asset and changes in implied volatility. Be prepared to adjust or close the trade as market conditions change or as you approach expiration. Some traders actively manage their spreads, potentially closing the position early if a significant portion of the maximum profit has been captured or if their outlook on the underlying asset changes. The bull call spread offers traders a way to express a bullish view with defined risk and potentially lower cost compared to outright long calls. By mastering this strategy, traders can expand their ability to profit from bullish market moves while maintaining better control over their risk exposure. Whether used as a standalone strategy or as part of a more complex options approach, bull call spreads provide a versatile tool for navigating bullish market conditions with a balanced risk-reward profile.

Bull Put Spread

The bull put spread is a popular options strategy that allows traders to profit from a bullish or neutral market outlook while generating immediate income. This vertical spread strategy involves simultaneously selling a put option at one strike price and buying another put option at a lower strike price, with both options having the same expiration date. The bull put spread is an excellent choice for traders who expect the underlying asset to remain stable or moderately increase in price, offering a way to potentially profit with limited risk. At its core, a bull put spread consists of two put options: one sold and one purchased. The trader sells a put option with a higher strike price and simultaneously buys a put option with a lower strike price. Both options have the same underlying asset and expiration date. The net result of this position is a credit, as the premium received from selling the higher strike put is greater than the premium paid for the lower strike put. This credit represents the maximum potential profit for the strategy.

The mechanics of a bull put spread can be understood by examining its components. The short put with the higher strike price generates income and provides the primary exposure to the bullish thesis. If the underlying asset remains above this strike price at expiration, this option expires worthless, allowing the trader to keep the entire premium. The long put with the lower strike price serves as protection, limiting the potential loss if the underlying asset declines significantly. The interplay between these two options creates a defined risk-reward profile that many traders find attractive, especially in markets where they expect stability or modest upside. Bull put spreads are particularly useful in several scenarios. When you have a neutral to moderately bullish outlook, expecting the underlying asset to remain stable or rise slightly, a bull put spread allows you to generate income while limiting your risk. This can be especially valuable in markets where you anticipate low volatility or gradual appreciation. Additionally, in low-yield environments, bull put spreads can provide a way to generate additional income on existing portfolio holdings or as a standalone strategy.

Another scenario where bull put spreads can be valuable is when you want to potentially acquire shares of a stock at a lower price than the current market value. If the underlying asset falls below the strike price of the short put at expiration, you may be obligated to purchase shares at that strike price. This can be an effective way to enter a long stock position at a discount, especially if you're comfortable owning the shares for the long term. Implementing a bull put spread involves several key steps, beginning with thorough market analysis. Start by identifying an underlying asset that you expect to remain stable or appreciate moderately. Consider both technical and fundamental factors that support your outlook. Look for assets with strong support levels, stable fundamentals, or catalysts that could prevent significant price declines. Once you've selected your underlying asset, choose an expiration date for your bull put spread. The choice of expiration will depend on your outlook and risk tolerance. Shorter-term expirations (30-45 days) are popular among many traders as they allow for more rapid time decay and frequent income generation opportunities. However, longer-term expirations can provide more premium, albeit with increased risk and capital commitment.

Selecting the appropriate strike prices is crucial in constructing your bull put spread. Choose a higher strike price for the put you'll sell and a lower strike price for the put you'll buy. The width between these strikes will determine your maximum potential loss and the amount of margin required to hold the position. A wider spread increases both the potential profit and the maximum loss, while a narrower spread limits both. Your choice should reflect your risk tolerance and your assessment of the underlying asset's likely price range. When you're ready to place the trade, enter the bull put spread as a single order, specifying both the sell and buy legs simultaneously. This ensures you get filled on both sides of the spread and avoids the risk of only partially completing the strategy. Most modern trading platforms allow you to enter spread orders directly, simplifying the process.

Before entering the trade, it's crucial to set a clear exit strategy. Determine in advance at what profit level you'll close the position and at what loss level you'll exit to limit your downside. Many traders aim to close the position when they've captured 50-75% of the maximum potential profit, as the risk-reward ratio becomes less favorable as you approach expiration. Additionally, have a plan for what you'll do if the underlying asset approaches or falls below the strike price of the short put as expiration nears. Once the trade is executed, monitor the position closely. Keep track of how the spread's value changes in relation to movements in the underlying asset and changes in implied volatility. Be prepared to adjust or close the trade as market conditions change or as you approach expiration. Some traders actively manage their spreads, potentially rolling the position to a later expiration date or adjusting strike prices if their outlook on the underlying asset changes.

It's important to be aware of the risks associated with bull put spreads, particularly the potential obligation to purchase shares of the underlying asset if it falls below the short put's strike price at expiration. Ensure you have sufficient capital to meet this obligation or a plan to close the position before expiration if needed. The bull put spread offers traders a way to generate income with defined risk in neutral to bullish market conditions. By mastering this strategy, traders can enhance their ability to profit from stable or moderately rising markets while maintaining control over their risk exposure. Whether used as a standalone income-generating strategy or as part of a more comprehensive options approach, bull put spreads provide a versatile tool for capitalizing on bullish market sentiment while offering a degree of downside protection.

Synthetic Long Stock

Synthetic long stock is an advanced options strategy that simulates the risk-reward profile of owning stock without actually purchasing the shares outright. This strategy involves simultaneously buying an at-the-money call option and selling an at-the-money put option with the same strike price and expiration date. The resulting position closely mimics the behavior of owning 100 shares of the underlying stock, offering traders a way to gain exposure to potential price appreciation with potentially lower capital requirements.

At its core, a synthetic long stock position consists of two options contracts: a long call and a short put. Both options typically have the same at-the-money strike price and the same expiration date. The long call provides upside potential, giving the trader the right to buy shares at the strike price. The short put creates an obligation to buy shares if the stock price falls below the strike price, simulating the downside risk of stock ownership. When combined, these two options create a position that responds to price changes in the underlying asset similarly to owning the stock outright. The mechanics of synthetic long stock can be understood by examining its components. The long call option gains value as the stock price rises above the strike price, providing unlimited upside potential. The short put option generates income from the premium received but exposes the trader to potential losses if the stock price falls below the strike price. The net cost or credit of establishing this position depends on the relative prices of the call and put options, which are influenced by factors such as implied volatility and time to expiration.

Synthetic long stock positions are particularly useful in several scenarios. One common application is when a trader wants exposure to a stock's potential upside but lacks the capital to purchase 100 shares outright. The synthetic long stock strategy often requires less capital than buying shares, especially when using margin, allowing traders to potentially gain exposure to more expensive stocks or larger positions than they could with direct stock purchases. Another scenario where synthetic long stock can be valuable is when a trader wants to gain long exposure to a stock but believes that options are currently underpriced relative to the stock. In this case, the synthetic long stock position might be established for a net credit, effectively being paid to take on a position similar to owning the stock.

Synthetic long stock can also be useful for traders who want to avoid certain risks or costs associated with direct stock ownership, such as dividend risk or borrowing costs for short sellers. By using options to create a stock-like position, traders can potentially navigate these issues more effectively. Implementing a synthetic long stock position involves several key steps, beginning with thorough market analysis. Start by identifying an underlying asset that you expect to appreciate in value. Consider both technical and fundamental factors that support your bullish outlook. Look for assets with strong growth potential, positive catalysts, or technical indicators suggesting an upward trend.

Once you've selected your underlying asset, choose an expiration date for your synthetic long stock position. The choice of expiration will depend on your investment horizon and risk tolerance. Longer-term expirations allow for more time for your bullish thesis to play out but come with higher options prices. Shorter-term expirations are less expensive but require the stock to move in your favor more quickly. Selecting the appropriate strike price is crucial in constructing your synthetic long stock position. Typically, at-the-money options are used, meaning the strike price is close to the current stock price. This provides the closest simulation of stock ownership. However, slight adjustments to the strike price can be made to create a small net credit or debit, depending on your specific goals and market outlook.

When you're ready to place the trade, enter the synthetic long stock position as a single order, specifying both the call purchase and put sale simultaneously. This ensures you get filled on both sides of the position and avoids the risk of only partially completing the strategy. Most advanced trading platforms allow you to enter complex orders directly, simplifying the process. Before entering the trade, it's crucial to set a clear exit strategy. Determine in advance at what profit level you'll close the position and at what loss level you'll exit to limit your downside. Consider setting stop-loss orders or using options strategies to hedge your position if the trade moves against you.

Once the trade is executed, monitor the position closely. Keep track of how the synthetic long stock position responds to changes in the underlying stock price, implied volatility, and time decay. Be prepared to adjust or close the trade as market conditions change or as you approach expiration. Some traders actively manage their positions, potentially rolling to later expirations or adjusting strike prices as needed. It's important to be aware of the risks associated with synthetic long stock positions, particularly the potential obligation to purchase shares if the stock price falls below the strike price of the short put. Ensure you have sufficient capital to meet this obligation or a plan to close the position before expiration if needed. Additionally, be mindful of any upcoming dividends, as the short put may be at risk of early assignment just before ex-dividend dates.

One key advantage of synthetic long stock is its flexibility. The position can be easily adjusted or closed by trading the individual options components. This allows for more dynamic management compared to owning stock outright. However, it also requires more active monitoring and a solid understanding of options mechanics. Synthetic long stock offers traders a way to gain exposure to potential stock price appreciation with potentially lower capital requirements and added flexibility. By mastering this strategy, traders can expand their ability to participate in bullish market moves while potentially optimizing their capital usage. Whether used as a standalone strategy or as part of a more comprehensive options approach, synthetic long stock provides a sophisticated tool for expressing bullish views on individual stocks or ETFs. However, due to its complexity and potential risks, it's best suited for experienced traders who are comfortable with advanced options strategies and active position management.

The Call Ratio Backspread

The call ratio backspread is an advanced options strategy that allows traders to profit from significant upward price movements while limiting downside risk. This strategy involves selling a number of at-the-money or slightly out-of-the-money call options and simultaneously buying a larger number of further out-of-the-money call options, all with the same expiration date. The ratio of long calls to short calls is typically 2:1 or 3:2, hence the term "ratio" in the strategy's name. At its core, a call ratio backspread consists of two components: short call options and a larger number of long call options. For example, in a 2:1 ratio, a trader might sell one at-the-money call and buy two out-of-the-money calls. The short call generates income and helps finance the purchase of the long calls. The goal is to create a position that has limited risk if the underlying asset doesn't move much or declines slightly, but offers substantial profit potential if the asset price rises significantly.

The mechanics of a call ratio backspread can be understood by examining its payoff structure. If the underlying asset's price remains below the strike price of the short call at expiration, all options expire worthless, and the trader keeps the small net credit (or pays the small net debit) from establishing the position. If the price rises moderately, the trader may face a limited loss as the short call becomes profitable while the long calls remain out of the money. However, if the price rises significantly, the profit from the extra long call(s) outpaces the loss on the short call, potentially leading to substantial gains. Call ratio backspreads are particularly useful in several scenarios. One common application is when a trader has a bullish outlook but wants to limit risk in case they're wrong. The strategy allows for significant profit potential if a large upward move occurs, while limiting the downside to a known amount if the stock stays flat or declines.

Another scenario where call ratio backspreads can be valuable is in anticipation of a potential significant event that could cause a large price movement. For example, ahead of earnings announcements, product launches, or other major corporate events, this strategy allows traders to position for a possible big upside move without risking too much if the event turns out to be a non-event or slightly negative. Call ratio backspreads can also be effective in markets where options are perceived to be underpriced relative to the potential for a large move. By buying more options than are sold, the strategy can take advantage of an expansion in implied volatility, which often accompanies significant price movements.

Implementing a call ratio backspread involves several key steps, beginning with thorough market analysis. Start by identifying an underlying asset that you believe has the potential for a significant upward move. Consider both technical and fundamental factors that support your outlook. Look for assets with upcoming catalysts, bullish chart patterns, or other indicators suggesting the possibility of a strong rally. Once you've selected your underlying asset, choose an expiration date for your call ratio backspread. The choice of expiration will depend on your outlook and the timing of any potential catalysts. Longer-term expirations provide more time for a big move to occur but are more expensive. Shorter-term expirations are cheaper but require the big move to happen more quickly. Selecting the appropriate strike prices is crucial in constructing your call ratio backspread. For the short call(s), choose a strike price at-the-money or slightly out-of-the-money. For the long calls, select a higher strike price that represents where you expect the underlying asset could move in a bullish scenario. The width between these strikes and the ratio of long to short calls will determine the risk-reward profile of the strategy.

When you're ready to place the trade, enter the call ratio backspread as a single order, specifying all legs simultaneously. This ensures you get filled on all components at prices that work together. Most advanced trading platforms allow you to enter complex spread orders directly. Before entering the trade, it's crucial to understand and plan for the potential outcomes. Calculate your maximum loss, which typically occurs when the underlying asset price is at or slightly above the short call strike at expiration. Determine your breakeven points and profit potential in various scenarios. Set clear exit criteria for both profit-taking and loss limitation.

Once the trade is executed, monitor the position closely. Keep track of how the backspread's value changes in relation to movements in the underlying asset and changes in implied volatility. Be prepared to adjust or close the trade as market conditions change or as you approach expiration. Some traders actively manage their backspreads, potentially adjusting the position if the underlying asset makes a significant move or if implied volatility changes dramatically. It's important to be aware of the risks associated with call ratio backspreads, particularly the potential for a maximum loss if the underlying asset price lands near the short call strike at expiration.

Additionally, early assignment on the short call(s) is a risk, especially if the underlying asset pays dividends.

One key advantage of the call ratio backspread is its ability to profit from both a significant price move and an increase in implied volatility. This makes it a powerful tool for traders who have a strong bullish view but want to limit their downside risk. The call ratio backspread offers traders a sophisticated way to position for significant upside potential while limiting risk. By carefully balancing short and long call options, traders can create a position that aligns with a bullish outlook while providing some downside protection. However, due to its complexity, this strategy is best suited for experienced options traders who are comfortable with advanced risk management techniques and active position monitoring. When used appropriately, the call ratio backspread can be a valuable addition to a trader's strategic toolkit, particularly in markets where large upward moves are anticipated.

Chapter Six

Strategies for Bearish Markets

"The stock market is filled with individuals who know the price of everything, but the value of nothing."
– Philip Fisher

In the dynamic world of financial markets, periods of bearish sentiment present unique challenges and opportunities for options traders. This chapter explores a range of strategies specifically designed to capitalize on downward market movements. Whether you're looking to profit from a strong downtrend, hedge a short stock position, or generate income in a falling market, the strategies outlined here provide a versatile toolkit for navigating bearish conditions. From straightforward long puts to more complex spread strategies, we'll examine how each approach can be tailored to suit different risk tolerances and market outlooks. As we delve into these bearish strategies, remember that successful options trading requires not just a directional view, but also a nuanced understanding of volatility, time decay, and risk management. Let's explore how to turn market declines into potential profits.

Bear Call Spread

The bear call spread is a popular options strategy that allows traders to profit from an anticipated decline in the price of the underlying asset while limiting both potential profit and risk. This vertical spread strategy involves simultaneously selling a call option at one strike price and buying another call option at a higher strike price, with both options having the same expiration date. The bear call spread is an excellent choice for traders who have a moderately bearish outlook and want to generate income while limiting their potential losses. At its core, a bear call spread consists of two call options: one sold and one purchased. The trader sells a call option with a lower strike price and simultaneously buys a call option with a higher strike price. Both options have the same underlying asset and expiration date. The net result of this position is a credit, as the premium received from selling the lower strike call is greater than the premium paid for the higher strike call. This credit represents the maximum potential profit for the strategy.

The mechanics of a bear call spread can be understood by examining its components. The short call with the lower strike price generates income and provides the primary exposure to the bearish thesis. If the underlying asset remains below this strike price at expiration, this option expires worthless, allowing the trader to keep the entire credit received. The long call with the higher strike price serves as protection, limiting the potential loss if the underlying asset rises significantly. The interplay between these two options creates a defined risk-reward profile that many traders find attractive, especially in markets where they expect moderate downside but want to limit their potential losses. Bear call spreads are particularly useful in several scenarios. When you have a neutral to moderately bearish outlook, expecting the underlying asset to remain stable or decline slightly, a bear call spread allows you to generate income while limiting your risk. This can be especially valuable in markets where you anticipate low volatility or gradual depreciation. Additionally, in low-yield environments, bear call spreads can provide a way to generate additional income on existing portfolio holdings or as a standalone strategy.

Another scenario where bear call spreads can be valuable is when you want to potentially profit from overvalued assets without the unlimited risk associated with short selling. The defined risk nature of the spread limits your potential loss to a known amount, making it a more conservative approach to expressing a bearish view. This is particularly appealing for traders who are wary of the potential for sharp upward spikes that can occur in bearish markets, often due to short squeezes or unexpected positive news. Bear call spreads can also be effective in high implied volatility environments. When options premiums are inflated due to high implied volatility, selling options becomes more attractive. The bear call spread allows you to sell an overpriced call option while simultaneously buying a cheaper call for protection, potentially benefiting from a contraction in volatility even if the underlying asset doesn't move as expected.

Implementing a bear call spread involves several key steps, beginning with thorough market analysis. Start by identifying an underlying asset that you expect to remain stable or depreciate moderately. Consider both technical and fundamental factors that support your bearish outlook. Look for assets with strong resistance levels, weakening fundamentals, or catalysts that could prevent significant price appreciation. This could involve analyzing financial statements, studying industry trends, or examining technical chart patterns that suggest a potential downturn. Once you've selected your underlying asset, choose an expiration date for your bear call spread. The choice of expiration will depend on your outlook and risk tolerance. Shorter-term expirations (30-45 days) are popular among many traders as they allow for more rapid time decay and frequent income generation opportunities. However, longer-term expirations can provide more premium, albeit with increased risk and capital commitment. Consider factors such as upcoming earnings reports, economic data releases, or other events that could impact the underlying asset when selecting your expiration date.

Selecting the appropriate strike prices is crucial in constructing your bear call spread. Choose a lower strike price for the call you'll sell and a higher strike price for the call you'll buy. The width between these strikes will determine your maximum potential loss and the amount of margin required to hold the position. A wider spread increases both the potential profit and the maximum loss, while a narrower spread limits both. Your choice should reflect your risk tolerance and your assessment of the underlying asset's likely price range. Some traders prefer to sell the call option at or slightly above the current market price to increase the likelihood of profiting from time decay, while others may choose a strike price further out-of-the-money for greater protection against upward movements.

When you're ready to place the trade, enter the bear call spread as a single order, specifying both the sell and buy legs simultaneously. This ensures you get filled on both sides of the spread and avoids the risk of only partially completing the strategy. Most modern trading platforms allow you to enter spread orders directly, simplifying the process. Be sure to use limit orders rather than market orders to ensure you receive the credit you're seeking for the spread. Before entering the trade, it's crucial to set a clear exit strategy. Determine in advance at what profit level you'll close the position and at what loss level you'll exit to limit your downside. Many traders aim to close the position when they've captured 50-75% of the maximum potential profit, as the risk-reward ratio becomes less favorable as you approach expiration. Additionally, have a plan for what you'll do if the underlying asset approaches or rises above the strike price of the short call as expiration nears. Some traders may choose to close the position early to avoid assignment risk, while others may be prepared to roll the spread to a later expiration date.

Once the trade is executed, monitor the position closely. Keep track of how the spread's value changes in relation to movements in the underlying asset and changes in implied volatility. Be prepared to adjust or close the trade as market conditions change or as you approach expiration. Some traders actively manage their spreads, potentially rolling the position to a later expiration date or adjusting strike prices if their outlook on the underlying asset changes. This active management can help maximize profits and minimize risks as market conditions evolve. It's important to be aware of the risks associated with bear call spreads, particularly the potential for early assignment on the short call option. This risk increases if the underlying asset rises above the short call's strike price, especially if it's a dividend-paying stock near an ex-dividend date. Ensure you have a plan to manage early assignment risk or the capital to fulfill the obligation if assigned. Early assignment can disrupt the spread and potentially lead to unexpected losses if not managed properly.

Another risk to consider is the impact of changes in implied volatility. While bear call spreads generally benefit from a decrease in implied volatility, a significant increase in volatility could negatively impact the position, even if the underlying asset moves in your favor. Understanding how volatility affects your spread can help you make better decisions about when to enter or exit the trade. One of the advantages of the bear call spread is its ability to profit from time decay. As the expiration date approaches, the time value of the options tends to decrease, which generally works in favor of the spread seller. This makes bear call spreads particularly attractive for traders who want to capitalize on the natural erosion of option premiums over time. When implementing bear call spreads, it's also important to consider the overall market environment. While these spreads can be effective in bearish or neutral markets, they may underperform in strongly bullish markets. Always consider the broader market context and how it might affect your specific trade.

The bear call spread offers traders a way to generate income with defined risk in neutral to bearish market conditions. By mastering this strategy, traders can enhance their ability to profit from stable or moderately declining markets while maintaining control over their risk exposure. Whether used as a standalone income-generating strategy or as part of a more comprehensive options approach, bear call spreads provide a versatile tool for capitalizing on bearish market sentiment while offering a degree of upside protection. As with any options strategy, success with bear call spreads requires thorough understanding, careful planning, and disciplined execution. Traders should practice implementing these spreads in a paper trading account before risking real capital. Additionally, it's valuable to analyze the performance of your bear call spreads over time, learning from both successful and unsuccessful trades to refine your approach. By incorporating bear call spreads into your trading arsenal, you can expand your ability to generate potential profits in various market conditions, particularly when you anticipate stability or downward price movements.

Bear Put Spread

The bear put spread is a popular options strategy that allows traders to profit from an anticipated decline in the price of the underlying asset while limiting both potential profit and risk. This vertical spread strategy involves simultaneously buying a put option at one strike price and selling another put option at a lower strike price, with both options having the same expiration date. The bear put spread is an excellent choice for traders who have a moderately bearish outlook and want to reduce the cost and risk associated with simply buying put options outright. At its core, a bear put spread consists of two put options: one purchased and one sold. The trader buys a put option with a higher strike price and simultaneously sells a put option with a lower strike price. Both options have the same underlying asset and expiration date. The net cost of this position (the debit) is the difference between the premium paid for the long put and the premium received for the short put. This structure allows traders to reduce the cost of taking a bearish position compared to buying a put option outright, as the premium received from selling the lower strike put partially offsets the cost of the higher strike put purchased.

The mechanics of a bear put spread can be understood by examining its components. The long put with the higher strike price provides the primary bearish exposure. As the stock price decreases below this strike price, this option gains intrinsic value. The short put with the lower strike price caps the potential profit but reduces the cost of the strategy. The interplay between these two options creates a defined risk-reward profile that many traders find attractive, especially in markets where they expect moderate downside but want to limit their potential losses. Bear put spreads are particularly useful in several scenarios. When you have a moderately bearish outlook, expecting the underlying asset to decline but unsure about significant downside potential, a bear put spread allows you to profit from a moderate decrease while limiting your risk. This can be especially valuable in markets where you anticipate steady decline rather than a dramatic crash. Additionally, in high volatility environments where options premiums are expensive, bear put spreads can provide a more cost-effective way to implement a bearish view compared to buying puts outright.

Another scenario where bear put spreads can be valuable is when you want to hedge a long stock position against potential losses. By implementing a bear put spread, you can protect your stock holdings from a moderate decline while limiting the cost of this protection compared to buying puts outright. This can be particularly appealing for investors who want to maintain their long-term stock positions but are concerned about short-term market volatility or specific risks to their holdings. Bear put spreads can also be effective in markets where you expect a decline but also anticipate high volatility. The spread nature of the strategy reduces the impact of changes in implied volatility compared to a single long put position. This can be advantageous in situations where you correctly predict the direction of the market move but might otherwise see your profits eroded by a decrease in implied volatility.

Implementing a bear put spread involves several key steps, beginning with thorough market analysis. Start by identifying an underlying asset that you expect to depreciate in value. Consider both technical and fundamental factors that support your bearish outlook. Look for assets with clear downward trends, weakening fundamentals, or catalysts that could drive price depreciation. This could involve analyzing financial statements, studying industry trends, or examining technical chart patterns that suggest a potential downturn. Once you've selected your underlying asset, choose an expiration date for your bear put spread. The choice of expiration will depend on your outlook and risk tolerance. Shorter-term expirations (30-45 days) are popular among many traders as they allow for more frequent trading opportunities and faster time decay of the short put. However, longer-term expirations can provide more time for your bearish thesis to play out, albeit at a higher cost. Consider factors such as upcoming earnings reports, economic data releases, or other events that could impact the underlying asset when selecting your expiration date.

Selecting the appropriate strike prices is crucial in constructing your bear put spread. Choose a higher strike price for the put you'll buy and a lower strike price for the put you'll sell. The width between these strikes will determine your maximum profit potential and the cost of the spread. A wider spread increases both the potential profit and the cost, while a narrower spread limits the potential profit but is less expensive to implement. Your choice should reflect your specific price target and risk tolerance. Some traders prefer to buy the put option at or slightly in-the-money to increase delta exposure, while selling the put further out-of-the-money to reduce the overall cost of the spread. When you're ready to place the trade, enter the bear put spread as a single order, specifying both the buy and sell legs simultaneously. This ensures you get filled on both sides of the spread and avoids the risk of only partially completing the strategy. Most modern trading platforms allow you to enter spread orders directly, simplifying the process. Be sure to use limit orders rather than market orders to ensure you don't overpay for the spread.

Before entering the trade, it's crucial to set a clear exit strategy. Determine in advance at what profit level you'll close the position and at what loss level you'll exit to limit your downside. Many traders aim to close the position when they've captured 50-75% of the maximum potential profit, as the risk-reward ratio becomes less favorable as you approach expiration. Additionally, have a plan for what you'll do if the underlying asset moves significantly in either direction. Some traders may choose to close the position early if their profit target is reached, while others may hold until expiration if the position is deep in-the-money.

Once the trade is executed, monitor the position closely. Keep track of how the spread's value changes in relation to movements in the underlying asset and changes in implied volatility. Be prepared to adjust or close the trade as market conditions change or as you approach expiration. Some traders actively manage their spreads, potentially rolling the position to a later expiration date or adjusting strike prices if their outlook on the underlying asset changes. This active management can help maximize profits and minimize risks as market conditions evolve. It's important to be aware of the risks associated with bear put spreads. While the maximum loss is limited to the initial debit paid for the spread, this loss can occur if the underlying asset price remains above the higher strike price at expiration. Additionally, if the price falls below the lower strike price, the profit is capped, meaning you could miss out on further gains if the asset continues to decline sharply.

Another factor to consider is the impact of time decay. While bear put spreads generally benefit from price movement in your favor, they are still subject to time decay, which affects both the long and short options. As expiration approaches, the rate of time decay accelerates, which can work against your position if the underlying asset doesn't move as expected. Changes in implied volatility can also affect the value of your bear put spread. Generally, an increase in implied volatility will benefit the spread (as it typically has positive vega), while a decrease in volatility will hurt it. However, the impact of volatility changes is usually less pronounced than it would be for a single long put position.

One advantage of the bear put spread is its defined risk-reward profile. Before entering the trade, you know exactly what your maximum potential profit and loss are. This can be particularly appealing for risk-averse traders or those who prefer to have precise control over their position's risk parameters. Bear put spreads can also be combined with other options strategies or used as part of a larger portfolio hedging strategy. For example, you might use bear put spreads on individual stocks or sectors that you expect to underperform, while maintaining long positions in other areas of the market. This allows for a more nuanced approach to expressing your market views and managing overall portfolio risk. When implementing bear put spreads, it's also important to consider the overall market environment. While these spreads can be effective in bearish markets, they may underperform in strongly bullish markets or in periods of low volatility. Always consider the broader market context and how it might affect your specific trade.

In conclusion, the bear put spread offers traders a way to express a bearish view with defined risk and potentially lower cost compared to outright long puts. By mastering this strategy, traders can expand their ability to profit from bearish market moves while maintaining better control over their risk exposure. Whether used as a standalone strategy or as part of a more comprehensive options approach, bear put spreads provide a versatile tool for capitalizing on downward price movements while offering a degree of cost reduction and risk management. As with any options strategy, success with bear put spreads requires thorough understanding, careful planning, and disciplined execution. Traders should practice implementing these spreads in a paper trading account before risking real capital. Additionally, it's valuable to analyze the performance of your bear put spreads over time, learning from both successful and unsuccessful trades to refine your approach.

By incorporating bear put spreads into your trading arsenal, you can expand your ability to generate potential profits in various market conditions, particularly when you anticipate downward price movements. This strategy allows you to tailor your risk and potential reward to your specific market outlook and risk tolerance, making it a valuable tool for both speculative traders and those looking to hedge existing positions. Remember that while bear put spreads can be an effective tool in bearish markets, they should be used as part of a well-rounded trading approach that includes thorough analysis, proper position sizing, and ongoing risk management. With practice and experience, bear put spreads can become a powerful addition to your options trading toolkit, allowing you to navigate bearish market conditions with greater precision and control.

Synthetic Short Stock

Synthetic short stock is an advanced options strategy that simulates the risk-reward profile of short selling a stock without actually borrowing and selling shares. This strategy involves simultaneously buying an at-the-money put option and selling an at-the-money call option with the same strike price and expiration date. The resulting position closely mimics the behavior of being short 100 shares of the underlying stock, offering traders a way to profit from price depreciation with potentially lower capital requirements and without the need to borrow shares. At its core, a synthetic short stock position consists of two options contracts: a long put and a short call. Both options typically have the same at-the-money strike price and the same expiration date. The long put provides downside potential, giving the trader the right to sell shares at the strike price. The short call creates an obligation to sell shares if the stock price rises above the strike price, simulating the upside risk of a short stock position. When combined, these two options create a position that responds to price changes in the underlying asset similarly to being short the stock outright.

The mechanics of synthetic short stock can be understood by examining its components. The long put option gains value as the stock price falls below the strike price, providing unlimited downside potential (limited only by the stock price reaching zero). The short call option generates income from the premium received but exposes the trader to potential losses if the stock price rises above the strike price. The net cost or credit of establishing this position depends on the relative prices of the put and call options, which are influenced by factors such as implied volatility and time to expiration. Synthetic short stock positions are particularly useful in several scenarios. One common application is when a trader wants to profit from an anticipated decline in a stock's price but faces difficulties or high costs associated with traditional short selling. This could be due to hard-to-borrow stocks with high borrowing fees, or in accounts that don't allow short selling. The synthetic short stock strategy provides a way to achieve a similar risk-reward profile without actually borrowing shares.

Another scenario where synthetic short stock can be valuable is when a trader wants to hedge a long stock position but doesn't want to sell the shares, perhaps for tax reasons or to maintain voting rights. By implementing a synthetic short stock position, the trader can effectively neutralize their exposure to price movements in the underlying stock without actually selling it. Synthetic short stock can also be useful for traders who believe that options are currently underpriced relative to the stock. In this case, the synthetic short stock position might be established for a net credit, effectively being paid to take on a position similar to shorting the stock. This can be particularly attractive in low implied volatility environments where options premiums are relatively cheap.

Implementing a synthetic short stock position involves several key steps, beginning with thorough market analysis. Start by identifying an underlying asset that you expect to depreciate in value. Consider both technical and fundamental factors that support your bearish outlook. Look for stocks with weakening financials, negative industry trends, technical breakdown patterns, or other catalysts that could drive the price lower. Once you've selected your underlying asset, choose an expiration date for your synthetic short stock position. The choice of expiration will depend on your investment horizon and risk tolerance. Longer-term expirations allow for more time for your bearish thesis to play out but come with higher options prices. Shorter-term expirations are less expensive but require the stock to move in your favor more quickly. Consider factors such as upcoming earnings reports or other significant events that could impact the stock price when selecting your expiration date. Selecting the appropriate strike price is crucial in constructing your synthetic short stock position. Typically, at-the-money options are used, meaning the strike price is close to the current stock price. This provides the closest simulation of short stock exposure. However, slight adjustments to the strike price can be made to create a small net credit or debit, depending on your specific goals and market outlook.

When you're ready to place the trade, enter the synthetic short stock position as a single order, specifying both the put purchase and call sale simultaneously. This ensures you get filled on both sides of the position and avoids the risk of only partially completing the strategy. Most advanced trading platforms allow you to enter complex orders directly, simplifying the process. Be sure to use limit orders to ensure you receive the desired net credit or pay the acceptable net debit for the position. Before entering the trade, it's crucial to set a clear exit strategy. Determine in advance at what profit level you'll close the position and at what loss level you'll exit to limit your downside. Consider setting stop-loss orders or using options strategies to hedge your position if the trade moves against you. Remember that while your potential profit is theoretically limited only by the stock price falling to zero, your potential loss is unlimited if the stock price rises significantly.

Once the trade is executed, monitor the position closely. Keep track of how the synthetic short stock position responds to changes in the underlying stock price, implied volatility, and time decay. Be prepared to adjust or close the trade as market conditions change or as you approach expiration. Some traders actively manage their positions, potentially rolling to later expirations or adjusting strike prices as needed to maintain their desired exposure. It's important to be aware of the risks associated with synthetic short stock positions. Unlike a traditional short stock position where you receive the proceeds from selling borrowed shares upfront, a synthetic short stock position doesn't provide any cash inflow (unless established for a net credit). This means you need to have sufficient margin or buying power in your account to cover potential losses if the stock price rises.

Another risk to consider is the potential for early assignment on the short call option. This risk increases if the stock price rises above the strike price, especially if it's a dividend-paying stock near an ex-dividend date. If assigned, you would be obligated to sell shares of the underlying stock at the strike price. Since you don't actually own the shares, this would result in a short stock position in your account. Be prepared to manage this risk by potentially exercising your long put or buying shares in the market to cover the assignment.

One key advantage of synthetic short stock is its flexibility. The position can be easily adjusted or closed by trading the individual options components. This allows for more dynamic management compared to a traditional short stock position. However, it also requires more active monitoring and a solid understanding of options mechanics. Synthetic short stock positions can also be impacted by changes in implied volatility. Generally, an increase in implied volatility will benefit the position (as it typically has positive vega due to the long put), while a decrease in volatility will hurt it. This is in contrast to a traditional short stock position, which is not directly affected by changes in implied volatility.

When using synthetic short stock, it's also important to consider the impact of dividends. If the underlying stock pays a dividend, the synthetic short position doesn't directly benefit from this (unlike a traditional short stock position where you would receive a credit for the dividend amount). However, the dividend expectation is typically priced into the options, affecting their relative values. In conclusion, synthetic short stock offers traders a way to gain exposure to potential stock price depreciation with potentially lower capital requirements and without the need to borrow shares. By mastering this strategy, traders can expand their ability to profit from bearish market moves or hedge long positions while potentially optimizing their capital usage. Whether used as a standalone strategy or as part of a more comprehensive options approach, synthetic short stock provides a sophisticated tool for expressing bearish views on individual stocks or ETFs. However, due to its complexity and potential risks, it's best suited for experienced traders who are comfortable with advanced options strategies and active position management.

The Long Put Calendar Spread

The long put calendar spread, also known as a horizontal put spread or time spread, is an advanced options strategy that involves simultaneously buying a longer-term put option and selling a shorter-term put option with the same strike price. This strategy allows traders to potentially profit from the passage of time and/or an increase in implied volatility while maintaining a bearish outlook on the underlying asset. The long put calendar spread is a versatile tool that can be used in various market conditions, making it an attractive choice for experienced options traders.

At its core, a long put calendar spread consists of two put options with the same strike price but different expiration dates. The trader buys a put option with a longer-term expiration and simultaneously sells a put option with a shorter-term expiration. The net result of this position is typically a debit, as the longer-term option usually costs more than the premium received from selling the shorter-term option. This initial cost represents the maximum potential loss for the strategy. The mechanics of a long put calendar spread can be understood by examining its components. The long put with the further expiration date provides the primary exposure to the underlying asset's price movement and changes in implied volatility. The short put with the nearer expiration date generates income and takes advantage of more rapid time decay. The goal is for the shorter-term option to expire worthless or lose value more quickly than the longer-term option, allowing the trader to potentially profit from the difference in time decay rates.

Long put calendar spreads are particularly useful in several scenarios. One common application is when a trader has a neutral to slightly bearish short-term outlook but expects a more significant decline in the longer term. In this case, the strategy allows the trader to potentially profit from time decay in the near term while maintaining exposure to a potential future price decline. Another scenario where long put calendar spreads can be valuable is in low implied volatility environments. When options are relatively cheap due to low implied volatility, establishing a long put calendar spread allows the trader to potentially benefit from an increase in implied volatility, which typically has a more pronounced effect on the longer-term option.

Long put calendar spreads can also be effective when a trader expects a period of consolidation or range-bound trading before a potential downward move. The strategy can profit from time decay during the consolidation phase and then benefit from the price decline once it occurs. Implementing a long put calendar spread involves several key steps, beginning with thorough market analysis. Start by identifying an underlying asset that aligns with your market outlook. Consider both short-term and longer-term factors that could influence the asset's price movement and volatility. Assess technical indicators, fundamental data, and any upcoming events that could impact your chosen underlying asset. Once you've selected your underlying asset, choose the expiration dates for your long put calendar spread. The choice of expirations will depend on your outlook and risk tolerance. Typically, the near-term option might have 30-45 days until expiration, while the longer-term option could be 60-90 days out or more. The wider the gap between expirations, the more expensive the spread will be to implement, but it will also provide more time for your thesis to play out.

Selecting the appropriate strike price is crucial in constructing your long put calendar spread. Typically, at-the-money or slightly out-of-the-money options are used for this strategy. The choice of strike price will depend on your specific outlook for the underlying asset and your risk tolerance. At-the-money options will be more expensive but provide a higher probability of profiting from time decay, while out-of-the-money options are cheaper but require a larger move in the underlying asset to become profitable. When you're ready to place the trade, enter the long put calendar spread as a single order, specifying both legs simultaneously. This ensures you get filled on both components of the spread and avoids the risk of only partially completing the strategy. Most modern trading platforms allow you to enter complex spread orders directly, simplifying the process.

Before entering the trade, it's crucial to set a clear exit strategy. Determine in advance at what profit level you'll close the position and at what loss level you'll exit to limit your downside. Many calendar spread traders aim to close the position when they've captured a certain percentage of the maximum potential profit, or when the short-term option approaches expiration. Having a predetermined stop-loss point can help limit losses if the trade moves against you. Once the trade is executed, monitor the position closely. Keep track of how the calendar spread's value changes in relation to movements in the underlying asset, changes in implied volatility, and the passage of time. Be prepared to adjust or close the trade as market conditions change or as you approach the near-term expiration. Some traders actively manage their calendar spreads, potentially rolling the short-term option to a new expiration date or adjusting strike prices as needed. It's important to be aware of the risks associated with long put calendar spreads. While the maximum loss is limited to the initial debit paid for the spread, the strategy can lose value quickly if the underlying asset moves significantly in either direction. A sharp upward move can cause both options to lose value, while a sharp downward move can increase the value of both options, potentially reducing the spread between them.

Another risk to consider is the impact of changes in implied volatility. Long put calendar spreads generally benefit from an increase in implied volatility, as this typically has a more significant impact on the longer-term option. However, a decrease in implied volatility can negatively affect the position, even if the underlying asset moves in your favor. One key advantage of the long put calendar spread is its flexibility. As the near-term expiration approaches, traders have several options for managing the position. They can close the entire spread, let the near-term option expire and hold the longer-term option, or roll the near-term option to a later expiration date. This flexibility allows traders to adapt to changing market conditions and adjust their strategy as their outlook evolves. Long put calendar spreads can also be combined with other options strategies or used as part of a larger portfolio hedging strategy. For example, they can be used in conjunction with long stock positions to provide a degree of downside protection while potentially generating income. When implementing long put calendar spreads, it's also important to consider the overall market environment. These spreads can be effective in various market conditions, but they tend to perform best when implied volatility is low and expected to increase. Always consider the broader market context and how it might affect your specific trade.

The long put calendar spread offers traders a sophisticated way to potentially profit from time decay and changes in implied volatility while maintaining a bearish outlook. By carefully selecting expiration dates and strike prices, traders can create positions that align closely with their market expectations. However, due to the strategy's complexity and sensitivity to various factors, it's best suited for experienced options traders who are comfortable with active position management and have a thorough understanding of options pricing dynamics.

The Put Ratio Backspread

The put ratio backspread is an advanced options strategy that allows traders to profit from significant downward price movements while limiting upside risk. This sophisticated approach involves selling a number of at-the-money or slightly out-of-the-money put options and simultaneously buying a larger number of further out-of-the-money put options, all with the same expiration date. The ratio of long puts to short puts is typically 2:1 or 3:2, hence the term "ratio" in the strategy's name. This configuration creates a position with unique risk-reward characteristics that can be particularly attractive in certain market conditions.

At its core, the mechanics of a put ratio backspread can be understood as a combination of short and long put options. The trader sells one or more put options at a higher strike price and buys a larger number of put options at a lower strike price. All options in the strategy share the same expiration date, which is crucial for maintaining the intended risk-reward profile. Interestingly, this position can often be established for a small debit or even a credit, depending on the specific strikes chosen and the prevailing market conditions. The goal is to create a position that has limited risk if the underlying asset doesn't move much or rises, but offers substantial profit potential if the asset price falls significantly.

The put ratio backspread is particularly useful in several scenarios. First and foremost, it's an excellent strategy for traders with a bearish outlook who expect a significant downward move in the underlying asset. Unlike a simple long put position, the ratio backspread allows for potentially greater profits if a large move occurs, while still limiting the potential loss if the bearish view proves incorrect. This risk-reward profile can be especially appealing in volatile markets or ahead of events that could trigger substantial price movements. Another scenario where put ratio backspreads shine is when a trader anticipates an increase in volatility. The strategy tends to benefit from volatility expansions, as the long puts (being further out-of-the-money) typically gain value faster than the short puts when implied volatility rises. This characteristic makes the put ratio backspread an interesting choice for traders who have a view not just on price direction, but also on the potential for market turbulence.

Risk management is another key reason traders might opt for a put ratio backspread. The strategy allows for significant downside profit potential while still maintaining a cap on potential losses. This can be particularly attractive for traders who want to express a strong bearish view but are wary of the unlimited risk associated with short selling stocks. In essence, the put ratio backspread offers a way to speculate on downside movements with a known and limited risk. The strategy can also serve as an alternative to short selling, especially in situations where borrowing stocks too short is difficult or expensive. By using options to create a similar risk profile, traders can potentially avoid some of the complications associated with short selling, such as recall risk or high borrowing costs.

Implementing a put ratio backspread involves several crucial steps, beginning with thorough market analysis. The trader must identify an underlying asset they believe has the potential for a significant price decline. This involves analyzing both technical and fundamental factors that support a bearish thesis. Traders might look for stocks showing technical breakdown patterns, companies with weakening financials, or sectors facing significant headwinds. It's also important to consider any upcoming events, such as earnings reports or economic announcements, that could potentially trigger a large price move. Once the underlying asset is selected, the next step is to choose an appropriate expiration date for the options. This decision should align with the trader's expected timeframe for the anticipated price move. If the bearish catalyst is an upcoming earnings report, for example, the trader might choose an expiration date shortly after the scheduled announcement. It's also crucial to consider options liquidity at different expiration dates, as more liquid options will generally offer better fill prices and easier exit opportunities.

Selecting the right strike prices is a critical aspect of constructing a put ratio backspread. The trader needs to choose a higher strike price for the puts they'll sell (typically at-the-money or slightly out-of-the-money) and a lower strike price for the puts they'll buy (further out-of-the-money). The width between these strikes will significantly affect the risk-reward profile of the trade. Wider spreads between the strikes will increase the potential profit if a large move occurs but will also typically increase the cost (or reduce the credit) of establishing the position. Determining the appropriate ratio is another key decision. While 2:1 and 3:2 are common ratios, the specific choice will depend on the trader's risk tolerance and market outlook. A higher ratio (more long puts relative to short puts) will increase the potential profit from a large downward move but will also typically increase the cost of the position. Traders must carefully consider how their chosen ratio affects the strategy's risk-reward profile and break-even points.

Before executing the trade, it's crucial to calculate and understand the potential outcomes. Traders should determine the maximum profit potential, maximum possible loss, and break-even points for the strategy. This analysis ensures that the risk-reward profile aligns with the trader's goals and risk tolerance. It's particularly important to understand that while the put ratio backspread can offer significant profit potential in a strong down move, it can also result in losses if the underlying asset price falls only slightly or remains relatively stable. When it comes time to place the trade, it's generally best to enter the put ratio backspread as a single order to ensure proper execution of all components at favorable prices. Using limit orders can help control the debit paid or credit received for the overall position. Given the complexity of the strategy, many brokers offer specific tools or order types to facilitate entering ratio spreads efficiently. As with any advanced options strategy, having a clear exit plan is essential. Traders should determine profit targets and stop-loss levels in advance, considering both percentage returns and specific price levels in the underlying asset. Some traders may opt for a scaled approach, taking partial profits at different levels if the trade moves in their favor.

Once the position is established, ongoing monitoring and management are crucial. Traders need to keep close track of movements in the underlying asset's price, as well as changes in implied volatility, which can significantly impact the position's value. Being prepared to adjust the position if market conditions change is an important aspect of successfully trading put ratio backspreads. As expiration approaches, traders must decide how to handle the position. This might involve closing the entire spread, letting some options expire while managing others, or rolling the position to a later expiration date if the bearish outlook remains intact but more time is needed.

While the put ratio backspread offers many advantages, it's important to be aware of its complexities and potential risks. The strategy's risk profile can change dramatically as the underlying asset's price moves, and the position can still result in significant losses if the price falls only slightly. Increases in implied volatility generally benefit this strategy, but sudden volatility spikes can lead to rapid changes in the position's value. Traders must also be mindful of margin requirements, especially if the position is established for a credit. The short put component of the strategy will typically require margin, and these requirements can increase if the position moves against the trader. Another consideration is the risk of early assignment on the short puts, particularly if they become in-the-money. While early assignment is generally rare, it's a risk that traders need to understand and be prepared to manage if it occurs.

The put ratio backspread is a powerful tool for experienced options traders looking to express a strongly bearish view while maintaining defined risk parameters. Its unique risk-reward profile can offer substantial profit potential in significant down moves while limiting losses in other scenarios. However, due to its complexity and the need for active management, this strategy is best suited for traders who have a solid understanding of options mechanics and are comfortable with advanced risk management techniques. When used appropriately, the put ratio backspread can be a valuable addition to a trader's strategic toolkit, particularly in markets where large downward moves are anticipated.

Chapter Seven

Strategies for Neutral Markets

"In investing, what is comfortable is rarely profitable."
– Robert Arnott

In the ever-changing landscape of financial markets, periods of stability or uncertainty can present unique challenges and opportunities for options traders. This chapter explores a range of strategies specifically designed to capitalize on sideways or range-bound market conditions. Whether you're looking to generate income, profit from time decay, or take advantage of volatility fluctuations without a strong directional bias, the strategies outlined here provide a versatile toolkit for navigating neutral market environments. From basic spreads to more complex multi-leg strategies, we'll examine how each approach can be tailored to suit different risk tolerances and market outlooks. As we delve into these neutral strategies, remember that successful options trading in sideways markets requires not just a lack of directional view, but also a nuanced understanding of time decay, volatility dynamics, and precise risk management. Let's explore how to potentially profit when the market seems to be going nowhere.

The Iron Condor

The iron condor is a popular neutral options strategy that allows traders to profit from a range-bound market while defining both potential profit and risk. This non-directional strategy involves simultaneously entering a bull put spread and a bear call spread on the same underlying asset with the same expiration date. The iron condor is favored by many options traders for its potential to generate income with limited risk, making it an attractive choice for those seeking to profit from time decay and stable market conditions.

At its core, an iron condor consists of four options contracts: two calls and two puts. The strategy is created by selling an out-of-the-money put, buying a further out-of-the-money put (creating a bull put spread), selling an out-of-the-money call, and buying a further out-of-the-money call (creating a bear call spread). All four options have the same expiration date but different strike prices. The name "iron condor" comes from the shape of the profit/loss diagram, which resembles a large-bodied bird with wings spread out. The basic mechanics of an iron condor can be understood by breaking down its components. The bull put spread (selling a put and buying a lower strike put) provides a bullish outlook, profiting if the underlying asset stays above the sold put's strike price. The bear call spread (selling a call and buying a higher strike call) provides a bearish outlook, profiting if the underlying asset stays below the sold call's strike price. When combined, these spreads create a range within which the strategy is profitable.

The maximum profit for an iron condor is achieved when the underlying asset's price at expiration is between the two sold options' strike prices. In this scenario, all four options expire worthless, and the trader keeps the entire net credit received when entering the position. The maximum loss is limited and occurs when the underlying asset's price at expiration is below the lower long put strike or above the higher long call strike. The risk is limited to the difference between the strike prices of either spread minus the net credit received. Iron condors are particularly useful in several scenarios. When you expect the underlying asset to remain relatively stable or trade within a specific range, an iron condor allows you to profit from this lack of significant price movement. This makes it an excellent strategy for markets that are consolidating or experiencing low volatility. Additionally, iron condors can be effective in high implied volatility environments, where option premiums are inflated. By selling options in these conditions, traders can potentially benefit from volatility contraction.

Another scenario where iron condors can be valuable is when you want to generate income in your portfolio without taking a strong directional view on the market. The strategy allows you to collect premium while maintaining a neutral outlook, which can be particularly attractive in uncertain market conditions or when you don't have a strong conviction about market direction. Implementing an iron condor involves several key steps, beginning with thorough market analysis. Start by identifying an underlying asset that you expect to remain relatively stable. This could be an individual stock, an ETF, or a market index. Consider both technical and fundamental factors that support your neutral outlook. Look for assets trading in a clear range or showing signs of low volatility. Additionally, examine the implied volatility of the options on the asset, as higher implied volatility can lead to more attractive premium collection opportunities.

Once you've selected your underlying asset, choose an expiration date for your iron condor. The choice of expiration will depend on your outlook and risk tolerance. Shorter-term expirations (30-45 days) are popular among many iron condor traders as they allow for more frequent trading opportunities and faster time decay. However, longer-term expirations can provide larger premiums and more time for adjustments if needed. Consider your trading style and the characteristics of the underlying asset when making this decision. Selecting the appropriate strike prices is crucial in constructing your iron condor. For the bull put spread component, choose a strike price for the short put that's below the current price of the underlying asset and has a low probability of being in-the-money at expiration. Then select a lower strike price for the long put, which will define your maximum loss on the put side. For the bear call spread component, choose a strike price for the short call that's above the current price of the underlying asset and has a low probability of being in-the-money at expiration. Then select a higher strike price for the long call, which will define your maximum loss on the call side.

The width between the strike prices in each spread will determine your maximum potential loss and the amount of margin required to hold the position. Wider spreads increase both the potential profit and the maximum loss. Consider your risk tolerance and account size when deciding on the width of your spreads. Many traders aim for a potential profit that's about one-third of the maximum loss, but this can vary based on market conditions and individual preferences. When you're ready to place the trade, enter the iron condor as a single order, specifying all four legs simultaneously. This ensures you get filled on all components of the spread and avoids the risk of only partially completing the strategy. Most modern trading platforms allow you to enter complex orders like iron condors directly, simplifying the process. However, it's still important to double-check all the details before submitting your order to avoid any costly mistakes.

Before entering the trade, it's crucial to set a clear exit strategy. Determine in advance at what profit level you'll close the position and at what loss level you'll exit to limit your downside. Many iron condor traders aim to close the position when they've captured 50-75% of the maximum potential profit, as the risk-reward ratio becomes less favorable as you approach expiration. Similarly, having a predetermined stop-loss point, such as a specific dollar amount or a certain percentage of the maximum loss, can help limit losses if the underlying asset moves outside your expected range.

Once the trade is executed, it's important to monitor and manage the position as it progresses. Keep track of how the iron condor's value changes in relation to movements in the underlying asset. Be prepared to adjust or close the trade as market conditions change or as you approach expiration. Some traders actively manage their iron condors, potentially rolling one side of the spread if the underlying asset moves too close to one of the short strikes. This active management approach can help maintain the desired risk profile and potentially increase the overall profitability of the strategy. It's important to be aware of potential early assignment risks, especially if the underlying asset pays dividends. While early assignment is generally rare for out-of-the-money options, it can occur if one of the short options becomes in-the-money. Understanding the dynamics of early assignment and how to manage such situations is important for any trader using spread strategies. Being prepared for this possibility can help you avoid surprises and manage your positions more effectively.

One of the key advantages of the iron condor is its ability to profit from time decay. As options approach expiration, they tend to lose value due to time decay (theta). Since the iron condor involves selling options, this time decay works in the trader's favor. However, this also means that the strategy can be sensitive to changes in implied volatility. A significant increase in implied volatility can negatively impact the position, even if the underlying asset remains within the desired range. Another factor to consider when trading iron condors is the impact of market volatility. While the strategy is designed to profit from low volatility environments, unexpected spikes in volatility can quickly turn a profitable position into a losing one. It's important to stay informed about potential market-moving events and to have a plan for managing your iron condors in case of sudden increases in volatility. Iron condors can also be adjusted to reflect different market outlooks. For example, if you have a slightly bullish bias, you might place the put spread closer to the current price of the underlying asset and the call spread further away. This creates an unbalanced or "skewed" iron condor that has a higher probability of profiting from small upward movements while still maintaining protection against large moves in either direction.

The iron condor is a versatile and powerful tool in the options trader's arsenal for neutral market conditions. It provides a way to potentially profit from range-bound markets while maintaining defined risk. By mastering this strategy, traders can expand their ability to generate income in various market conditions, particularly when volatility is low or when they don't have a strong directional bias. Whether used as a standalone strategy or as part of a more complex options approach, iron condors offer traders a flexible and potentially effective way to navigate neutral market conditions. However, like all options strategies, success with iron condors requires thorough understanding, careful planning, and disciplined execution.

The Iron Butterfly

The iron butterfly is an advanced options strategy that allows traders to profit from a highly stable or range-bound market while defining both potential profit and risk. This neutral strategy combines elements of both the iron condor and the butterfly spread, creating a position that benefits from time decay and low volatility. The iron butterfly is favored by experienced options traders for its potential to generate significant returns when the underlying asset remains close to a specific price point.

At its core, an iron butterfly consists of four options contracts: two puts and two calls, all with the same expiration date but three different strike prices. The strategy is created by selling an at-the-money put and an at-the-money call (with the same strike price), while simultaneously buying an out-of-the-money put and an out-of-the-money call. The resulting position resembles a combination of a short straddle and a long strangle, with the name "iron butterfly" reflecting its profit/loss diagram shape and its defined risk nature. The basic mechanics of an iron butterfly can be understood by examining its components. The short at-the-money put and call (often referred to as the "body" of the butterfly) generate income and benefit from time decay. These short options provide the main profit potential if the underlying asset remains near the middle strike price. The long out-of-the-money put and call (the "wings" of the butterfly) serve to limit the potential losses if the underlying asset moves significantly in either direction.

The maximum profit for an iron butterfly is achieved when the underlying asset's price at expiration is exactly at the middle strike price (where the short options were sold). In this ideal scenario, all options except the short at-the-money options expire worthless, and the trader keeps the entire net credit received when entering the position. The maximum loss is limited and occurs when the underlying asset's price at expiration is below the lower long put strike or above the higher long call strike. The risk is limited to the difference between the middle strike and either wing strike, minus the net credit received. Iron butterflies are particularly useful in several scenarios. When you have a strong conviction that the underlying asset will remain very close to a specific price point, an iron butterfly allows you to potentially profit significantly from this lack of movement. This makes it an excellent strategy for markets that are highly range-bound or experiencing extremely low volatility. Additionally, iron butterflies can be effective in high implied volatility environments, where option premiums are inflated. By selling options in these conditions, traders can potentially benefit from both time decay and volatility contraction.

Another scenario where iron butterflies can be valuable is when you want to generate income in your portfolio with a very specific price target in mind. The strategy allows you to collect premium while expressing a highly focused neutral outlook, which can be particularly attractive when you have a strong conviction about a stock's fair value or a key technical level that you expect to hold. Implementing an iron butterfly involves several key steps, beginning with thorough market analysis. Start by identifying an underlying asset that you expect to remain very stable around a specific price point. This could be an individual stock, an ETF, or a market index. Consider both technical and fundamental factors that support your neutral outlook. Look for assets trading in a tight range or showing signs of low volatility. Additionally, examine the implied volatility of the options on the asset, as higher implied volatility can lead to more attractive premium collection opportunities. Once you've selected your underlying asset, choose an expiration date for your iron butterfly. The choice of expiration will depend on your outlook and risk tolerance. Shorter-term expirations (30-45 days) are popular among many iron butterfly traders as they allow for more frequent trading opportunities and faster time decay. However, longer-term expirations can provide larger premiums and more time for adjustments if needed. Consider your trading style and the characteristics of the underlying asset when making this decision.

Selecting the appropriate strike prices is crucial in constructing your iron butterfly. Choose an at-the-money strike price for the short put and call, which should be as close as possible to the current price of the underlying asset. Then select lower and higher strike prices for the long put and call, respectively. These "wing" strikes define your maximum loss and should be equidistant from the middle strike. The width between the middle strike and the wing strikes will determine your maximum potential loss and the amount of margin required to hold the position. Wider spreads increase both the potential profit and the maximum loss. Consider your risk tolerance and account size when deciding on the width of your spreads. When you're ready to place the trade, enter the iron butterfly as a single order, specifying all four legs simultaneously. This ensures you get filled on all components of the spread and avoids the risk of only partially completing the strategy. Most modern trading platforms allow you to enter complex orders like iron butterflies directly, simplifying the process. However, it's still important to double-check all the details before submitting your order to avoid any costly mistakes.

Before entering the trade, it's crucial to set a clear exit strategy. Determine in advance at what profit level you'll close the position and at what loss level you'll exit to limit your downside. Many iron butterfly traders aim to close the position when they've captured 50-75% of the maximum potential profit, as the risk-reward ratio becomes less favorable as you approach expiration. Similarly, having a predetermined stop-loss point, such as a specific dollar amount or a certain percentage of the maximum loss, can help limit losses if the underlying asset moves outside your expected range. Once the trade is executed, it's important to monitor and manage the position actively. Keep track of how the iron butterfly's value changes in relation to movements in the underlying asset. Be prepared to adjust or close the trade as market conditions change or as you approach expiration. Some traders actively manage their iron butterflies, potentially rolling the position or adjusting the strikes if the underlying asset moves away from the middle strike price. This active management approach can help maintain the desired risk profile and potentially increase the overall profitability of the strategy.

It's important to be aware of potential early assignment risks, especially for the short options in the strategy. While early assignment is generally rare for at-the-money options, it can occur if one of the short options becomes significantly in-the-money. Understanding the dynamics of early assignment and how to manage such situations is important for any trader using spread strategies. Being prepared for this possibility can help you avoid surprises and manage your positions more effectively. One of the key advantages of the iron butterfly is its ability to profit significantly from time decay when the underlying asset remains stable. As options approach expiration, they tend to lose value due to time decay (theta). Since the iron butterfly involves selling at-the-money options, which have the highest theta, this time decay can work strongly in the trader's favor. However, this also means that the strategy can be sensitive to changes in implied volatility. A significant increase in implied volatility can negatively impact the position, even if the underlying asset remains near the middle strike price.

Another factor to consider when trading iron butterflies is the impact of market volatility. While the strategy is designed to profit from extremely low volatility environments, unexpected spikes in volatility can quickly turn a profitable position into a losing one. It's important to stay informed about potential market-moving events and to have a plan for managing your iron butterflies in case of sudden increases in volatility. The iron butterfly is a sophisticated tool in the options trader's arsenal for highly focused neutral market conditions. It provides a way to potentially profit significantly from range-bound markets while maintaining defined risk. By mastering this strategy, traders can expand their ability to generate income in specific market conditions, particularly when they have a strong conviction about an asset's stability around a particular price point. However, due to its complexity and sensitivity to price movements, the iron butterfly is best suited for experienced options traders who are comfortable with active position management and have a thorough understanding of options pricing dynamics.

The Long Straddle

The long straddle is a popular options strategy that allows traders to profit from significant price movements in either direction, without needing to predict whether the move will be up or down. This non-directional strategy involves simultaneously buying a call option and a put option with the same strike price and expiration date on the same underlying asset. The long straddle is particularly useful when a trader anticipates a large price move but is unsure of the direction, making it a valuable tool for volatile markets or ahead of significant events that could impact an asset's price. At its core, a long straddle consists of two options contracts: a call and a put. Both options have the same underlying asset, strike price, and expiration date. The trader buys both options, which means they're paying two premiums and taking on the role of the option holder for both contracts. This dual purchase gives the trader the right, but not the obligation, to both buy (via the call) and sell (via the put) the underlying asset at the strike price before or at expiration.

The basic mechanics of a long straddle can be understood by examining its components. The long call option gives the trader the right to buy the underlying asset at the strike price. As the asset's price increases above the strike price plus the total premium paid, this option becomes profitable. Conversely, the long put option gives the trader the right to sell the underlying asset at the strike price. As the asset's price decreases below the strike price minus the total premium paid, this option becomes profitable. The combination of these two options creates a position that can profit from a move in either direction, as long as the move is large enough to overcome the total cost of the premiums. The profit potential for a long straddle is theoretically unlimited on the upside (due to the call option) and limited only by the underlying asset reaching zero on the downside (due to the put option). The maximum loss is limited to the total premium paid for both options, which occurs if the underlying asset's price at expiration is exactly at the strike price, causing both options to expire worthless. The break-even points for a straddle are calculated by adding and subtracting the total premium paid from the strike price.

Long straddles are particularly useful in several scenarios. One of the most common applications is when a trader anticipates a significant market-moving event but is uncertain about the direction of the move. This could be ahead of earnings announcements, regulatory decisions, clinical trial results for pharmaceutical companies, or any other event that could cause a large price swing. By implementing a long straddle, the trader can potentially profit regardless of whether the news is positive or negative, as long as the resulting price move is large enough. Another scenario where long straddles can be valuable is during periods of low volatility that are expected to be followed by increased volatility. If a trader believes that an asset has been trading in a tight range but is likely to break out in either direction, a long straddle can provide exposure to this anticipated increase in volatility. This makes straddles a popular choice for traders who have a view on volatility rather than on price direction.

Long straddles can also be used as a hedging tool in certain situations. For example, if a trader has a large position in an underlying asset and wants to protect against potential losses without giving up the possibility of gains, a long straddle can provide this two-way protection. While this is generally a more expensive form of hedging compared to simply buying a protective put, it allows the trader to maintain full upside potential. Implementing a long straddle involves several key steps, beginning with thorough market analysis. Start by identifying an underlying asset that you expect to experience a significant price move. This could be an individual stock, an ETF, or a market index. Consider both technical and fundamental factors that support your expectation of increased volatility or a large price move. Look for assets with upcoming events that could cause significant price swings, or those that have been trading in a tight range and may be due for a breakout.

Once you've selected your underlying asset, choose an expiration date for your long straddle. The choice of expiration will depend on your outlook and the timing of any anticipated events. If you're trading a straddle around a specific event, such as an earnings announcement, you'll typically want to choose an expiration date shortly after the event. For more general volatility plays, longer-term expirations might be appropriate. Keep in mind that longer-term options will be more expensive but will give your thesis more time to play out. Selecting the appropriate strike price is crucial in constructing your long straddle. Typically, at-the-money options are used, meaning the strike price is as close as possible to the current price of the underlying asset. This provides a balanced exposure to moves in either direction. However, some traders might choose to implement a slightly bullish or bearish bias by selecting a strike price slightly above or below the current asset price.

When you're ready to place the trade, enter the long straddle as a single order, specifying both the call and put legs simultaneously. This ensures you get filled on both options at the same time, avoiding any risk of market movement between separate orders. Most modern trading platforms allow you to enter straddle orders directly, simplifying the process. However, it's still important to double-check all the details before submitting your order to avoid any costly mistakes. Before entering the trade, it's crucial to set a clear exit strategy. Determine in advance at what profit level you'll close the position and at what loss level you'll exit to limit your downside. Many straddle traders aim to close the position if they achieve a certain percentage of profit, such as 50% or 100% of the initial investment. Similarly, having a predetermined stop-loss point can help limit losses if the underlying asset fails to make the anticipated move.

Once the trade is executed, it's important to monitor and manage the position actively. Keep track of how the straddle's value changes in relation to movements in the underlying asset and changes in implied volatility. Be prepared to adjust or close the trade as market conditions change or as you approach expiration. Some traders actively manage their straddles, potentially closing one side of the position if the underlying asset makes a significant move in one direction, leaving the other side open for potential further gains. It's important to be aware of the risks associated with long straddles. While the maximum loss is limited to the premium paid, this can still be a significant amount, especially for longer-term or higher volatility options. Additionally, time decay works against long straddle positions, eroding their value as expiration approaches. This means that even if your directional view is correct, you may still lose money if the move doesn't happen quickly enough or isn't large enough to overcome the impact of time decay.

Changes in implied volatility can also significantly affect the value of a long straddle. Generally, an increase in implied volatility will benefit the position, while a decrease will hurt it. This sensitivity to volatility changes means that a straddle's value can fluctuate even if the underlying asset's price remains unchanged. The long straddle offers traders a way to potentially profit from significant price movements without needing to predict the direction. It's a powerful tool for trading around major events or in anticipation of increased volatility. However, it requires careful timing and a significant move in the underlying asset to be profitable. Traders must weigh the potential for large profits against the high cost and the risk of losing the entire premium paid if the anticipated move doesn't materialize. When used appropriately, long straddles can be a valuable addition to a trader's strategic toolkit, particularly in markets where large moves are anticipated but the direction is uncertain.

The Long Strangle

The long strangle is a popular options strategy that, like the long straddle, allows traders to profit from significant price movements in either direction without needing to predict whether the move will be up or down. However, the strangle differs from the straddle in its structure and risk-reward profile. This non-directional strategy involves simultaneously buying an out-of-the-money call option and an out-of-the-money put option with the same expiration date on the same underlying asset. The long strangle is particularly useful when a trader anticipates a large price move but is unsure of the direction and wants a less expensive alternative to the straddle.

At its core, a long strangle consists of two options contracts: an out-of-the-money call and an out-of-the-money put. Both options have the same underlying asset and expiration date, but different strike prices. The trader buys both options, which means they're paying two premiums and taking on the role of the option holder for both contracts. This dual purchase gives the trader the right, but not the obligation, to both buy (via the call) and sell (via the put) the underlying asset at their respective strike prices before or at expiration. The basic mechanics of a long strangle can be understood by examining its components. The long call option gives the trader the right to buy the underlying asset at the higher strike price. As the asset's price increases above this strike price plus the total premium paid, this option becomes profitable. Conversely, the long put option gives the trader the right to sell the underlying asset at the lower strike price. As the asset's price decreases below this strike price minus the total premium paid, this option becomes profitable. The combination of these two out-of-the-money options creates a position that can profit from a move in either direction, as long as the move is large enough to overcome the total cost of the premiums.

The profit potential for a long strangle is theoretically unlimited on the upside (due to the call option) and limited only by the underlying asset reaching zero on the downside (due to the put option). The maximum loss is limited to the total premium paid for both options, which occurs if the underlying asset's price at expiration is between the two strike prices, causing both options to expire worthless. The break-even points for a strangle are calculated by adding the total premium paid to the call strike price for the upside breakeven, and subtracting the total premium paid from the put strike price for the downside breakeven. Long strangles are particularly useful in several scenarios. One of the most common applications is when a trader anticipates a significant market-moving event but is uncertain about the direction of the move and wants a less expensive alternative to a straddle. This could be ahead of earnings announcements, regulatory decisions, economic data releases, or any other event that could cause a large price swing. By implementing a long strangle, the trader can potentially profit regardless of whether the news is positive or negative, as long as the resulting price move is large enough to surpass one of the break-even points.

Another scenario where long strangles can be valuable is during periods of low volatility that are expected to be followed by increased volatility. If a trader believes that an asset has been trading in a tight range but is likely to break out in either direction, a long strangle can provide exposure to this anticipated increase in volatility at a lower cost than a straddle. This makes strangles a popular choice for traders who have a view on volatility rather than on price direction and are willing to accept a larger required price move for profitability in exchange for lower upfront costs. Long strangles can also be used as a hedging tool in certain situations. For example, if a trader has a large position in an underlying asset and wants to protect against potential extreme losses without giving up too much upside potential, a long strangle can provide this two-way protection at a lower cost than a straddle. While this is still a more expensive form of hedging compared to simply buying a protective put, it allows the trader to maintain full upside potential beyond the call strike price.

Implementing a long strangle involves several key steps, beginning with thorough market analysis. Start by identifying an underlying asset that you expect to experience a significant price move. This could be an individual stock, an ETF, or a market index. Consider both technical and fundamental factors that support your expectation of increased volatility or a large price move. Look for assets with upcoming events that could cause significant price swings, or those that have been trading in a tight range and may be due for a breakout. Once you've selected your underlying asset, choose an expiration date for your long strangle. The choice of expiration will depend on your outlook and the timing of any anticipated events. If you're trading a strangle around a specific event, such as an earnings announcement, you'll typically want to choose an expiration date shortly after the event. For more general volatility plays, longer-term expirations might be appropriate. Keep in mind that longer-term options will be more expensive but will give your thesis more time to play out.

Selecting the appropriate strike prices is crucial in constructing your long strangle. Unlike a straddle, which typically uses at-the-money options, a strangle uses out-of-the-money options. You'll need to choose a call strike price above the current asset price and a put strike price below it. The wider the spread between these strike prices, the less expensive the strangle will be to implement, but the larger the price move required for profitability. Your choice of strike prices should reflect your assessment of the potential magnitude of the price move and your risk tolerance. When you're ready to place the trade, enter the long strangle as a single order, specifying both the call and put legs simultaneously. This ensures you get filled on both options at the same time, avoiding any risk of market movement between separate orders. Most modern trading platforms allow you to enter strangle orders directly, simplifying the process. However, it's still important to double-check all the details before submitting your order to avoid any costly mistakes.

Before entering the trade, it's crucial to set a clear exit strategy. Determine in advance at what profit level you'll close the position and at what loss level you'll exit to limit your downside. Many strangle traders aim to close the position if they achieve a certain percentage of profit, such as 50% or 100% of the initial investment. Similarly, having a predetermined stop-loss point can help limit losses if the underlying asset fails to make the anticipated move. Once the trade is executed, it's important to monitor and manage the position actively. Keep track of how the strangle's value changes in relation to movements in the underlying asset and changes in implied volatility. Be prepared to adjust or close the trade as market conditions change or as you approach expiration. Some traders actively manage their strangles, potentially closing one side of the position if the underlying asset makes a significant move in one direction, leaving the other side open for potential further gains.

It's important to be aware of the risks associated with long strangles. While the maximum loss is limited to the premium paid, the strategy requires a larger move in the underlying asset to be profitable compared to a straddle. Traders must weigh the lower cost and potential for large profits against the higher break even points and the risk of losing the entire premium paid if the anticipated move doesn't materialize. The long strangle offers traders a way to potentially profit from significant price movements without needing to predict the direction, and at a lower cost than a straddle. By mastering this strategy, traders can expand their ability to navigate uncertain market conditions and capitalize on events that are expected to cause large price swings, while managing their risk through lower upfront costs. However, like all options strategies, success with long strangles requires thorough understanding, careful planning, and disciplined execution.

The Short Straddle

The short straddle is an advanced options strategy that allows traders to profit from a lack of significant price movement in the underlying asset. This neutral strategy involves simultaneously selling a call option and a put option with the same strike price and expiration date on the same underlying asset. The short straddle is designed to take advantage of time decay and potentially profit from overpriced options in high implied volatility environments. However, it's important to note that this strategy comes with unlimited risk potential and is generally considered suitable only for experienced options traders. At its core, a short straddle consists of two options contracts: a short call and a short put. Both options have the same underlying asset, strike price, and expiration date. The trader sells both options, which means they're receiving two premiums and taking on the role of the option writer for both contracts. This dual sale obligates the trader to buy the underlying asset (if the put is exercised) or sell the underlying asset (if the call is exercised) at the strike price if the options are exercised by their respective holders.

The basic mechanics of a short straddle can be understood by examining its components. The short call option obligates the trader to sell the underlying asset at the strike price if the option is exercised. As the asset's price increases above the strike price plus the total premium received, this option position becomes unprofitable. Conversely, the short put option obligates the trader to buy the underlying asset at the strike price if the option is exercised. As the asset's price decreases below the strike price minus the total premium received, this option position becomes unprofitable. The combination of these two short options creates a position that can profit if the underlying asset remains close to the strike price, but can incur significant losses if the asset makes a large move in either direction. The maximum profit for a short straddle is limited to the total premium received for both options, which occurs if the underlying asset's price at expiration is exactly at the strike price, causing both options to expire worthless. The potential loss, however, is theoretically unlimited on the upside (due to the short call) and limited only by the underlying asset reaching zero on the downside (due to the short put). The break-even points for a short straddle are calculated by adding and subtracting the total premium received from the strike price.

Short straddles are particularly useful in several specific scenarios. One common application is when a trader expects the underlying asset to remain relatively stable in price. This could be during periods of low market volatility or when an asset is trading in a tight range. By implementing a short straddle, the trader can potentially profit from time decay as long as the asset price doesn't move significantly. Another scenario where short straddles can be valuable is when implied volatility is unusually high. Options tend to be overpriced when implied volatility is elevated, and selling options in these conditions can be profitable if volatility subsequently decreases. This makes short straddles a potential strategy for traders who believe that the market is overestimating the likelihood of a large price move. Short straddles can also be used as part of more complex options strategies or in conjunction with other positions. For example, a trader might use a short straddle to generate income on a long stock position, effectively creating a combination strategy that profits if the stock remains stable or rises moderately.

Implementing a short straddle involves several key steps, beginning with thorough market analysis. Start by identifying an underlying asset that you expect to remain stable in price. This could be an individual stock, an ETF, or a market index. Consider both technical and fundamental factors that support your expectation of price stability. Look for assets trading in a tight range or showing signs of low historical volatility. Additionally, examine the implied volatility of the options on the asset, as higher implied volatility can lead to more attractive premium collection opportunities. Once you've selected your underlying asset, choose an expiration date for your short straddle. The choice of expiration will depend on your outlook and risk tolerance. Shorter-term expirations (30-45 days) are popular among many straddle sellers as they allow for more rapid time decay. However, longer-term expirations can provide larger premiums. Consider your trading style and the characteristics of the underlying asset when making this decision.

Selecting the appropriate strike price is crucial in constructing your short straddle. Typically, at-the-money options are used, meaning the strike price is as close as possible to the current price of the underlying asset. This provides the highest premium and the greatest profit potential if the asset remains stable. However, it also presents the highest risk if the asset price moves significantly. When you're ready to place the trade, enter the short straddle as a single order, specifying both the call and put legs simultaneously. This ensures you get filled on both options at the same time, avoiding any risk of market movement between separate orders. Most modern trading platforms allow you to enter straddle orders directly, simplifying the process. However, it's still important to double-check all the details before submitting your order to avoid any costly mistakes.

Before entering the trade, it's crucial to set a clear exit strategy. Determine in advance at what profit level you'll close the position and at what loss level you'll exit to limit your downside. Many short straddle traders aim to close the position when they've captured a certain percentage of the maximum potential profit, such as 50% or 75%. Setting a maximum acceptable loss is particularly important for short straddles due to the unlimited risk potential. Once the trade is executed, it's critical to monitor and manage the position actively. Keep track of how the straddle's value changes in relation to movements in the underlying asset and changes in implied volatility. Be prepared to adjust or close the trade as market conditions change or as you approach expiration. Some traders actively manage their short straddles, potentially rolling the position to a later expiration date or adjusting strike prices if the underlying asset moves away from the initial strike price.

It's extremely important to be aware of the risks associated with short straddles. The potential for unlimited losses means that risk management is crucial. Many traders use stop-loss orders or options to hedge their position. Additionally, be aware of the risk of early assignment, especially if the underlying asset pays dividends or if one side of the straddle becomes deeply in-the-money. Changes in implied volatility can significantly affect the value of a short straddle. Generally, a decrease in implied volatility will benefit the position, while an increase will hurt it. This sensitivity to volatility changes means that a straddle's value can fluctuate even if the underlying asset's price remains unchanged. The short straddle offers traders a way to potentially profit from price stability and time decay. However, it comes with significant risks and requires careful management. It's best suited for experienced options traders who have a thorough understanding of options mechanics, strong risk management skills, and the ability to monitor and adjust positions actively. When used appropriately, short straddles can be a valuable tool for generating income in stable market conditions, but they should be approached with caution and a full appreciation of their risk profile.

Chapter Eight

Strategies for Volatile Markets

"Volatility is a measure of how much the stock price fluctuates."
– John C. Bogle

In the dynamic world of financial markets, periods of high volatility present both significant challenges and unique opportunities for options traders. This chapter explores a range of strategies specifically designed to capitalize on increased market turbulence. Whether you're looking to profit from large price swings, hedge against uncertainty, or take advantage of inflated option premiums, the strategies outlined here provide a versatile toolkit for navigating volatile market conditions. From simple long volatility plays to more complex multi-leg strategies, we'll examine how each approach can be tailored to suit different risk tolerances and market outlooks. As we delve into these volatility-focused strategies, remember that successful options trading in turbulent markets requires not just a view on direction, but also a nuanced understanding of volatility dynamics, time decay, and precise risk management. Let's explore how to potentially turn market turbulence into trading opportunities.

The Long Straddle

The long straddle is a popular options strategy that allows traders to profit from significant price movements in either direction, without needing to predict whether the move will be up or down. This non-directional strategy involves simultaneously buying a call option and a put option with the same strike price and expiration date on the same underlying asset. The long straddle is particularly valuable in volatile markets or ahead of events that could cause large price swings, making it a key tool for traders looking to capitalize on market turbulence. At its core, a long straddle consists of two options contracts: a call and a put. Both options have the same underlying asset, strike price, and expiration date. The trader buys both options, which means they're paying two premiums and taking on the role of the option holder for both contracts. This dual purchase gives the trader the right, but not the obligation, to both buy (via the call) and sell (via the put) the underlying asset at the strike price before or at expiration.

The basic mechanics of a long straddle can be understood by examining its components. The long call option gives the trader the right to buy the underlying asset at the strike price. As the asset's price increases above the strike price plus the total premium paid, this option becomes profitable. Conversely, the long put option gives the trader the right to sell the underlying asset at the strike price. As the asset's price decreases below the strike price minus the total premium paid, this option becomes profitable. The combination of these two options creates a position that can profit from a move in either direction, as long as the move is large enough to overcome the total cost of the premiums.

The profit potential for a long straddle is theoretically unlimited on the upside (due to the call option) and limited only by the underlying asset reaching zero on the downside (due to the put option). The maximum loss is limited to the total premium paid for both options, which occurs if the underlying asset's price at expiration is exactly at the strike price, causing both options to expire worthless. The break-even points for a straddle are calculated by adding and subtracting the total premium paid from the strike price. Long straddles are particularly useful in several scenarios common to volatile markets. One of the most frequent applications is when a trader anticipates a significant market-moving event but is uncertain about the direction of the move. This could be ahead of earnings announcements, Federal Reserve decisions, major economic data releases, or geopolitical events that could cause large price swings. By implementing a long straddle, the trader can potentially profit regardless of whether the news is positive or negative, as long as the resulting price move is large enough.

Another scenario where long straddles shine in volatile markets is when a trader expects an increase in volatility itself. If a trader believes that market turbulence is about to increase significantly, a long straddle can provide exposure to this anticipated spike in volatility. This is because option prices tend to increase when volatility rises, potentially benefiting both legs of the straddle even if the underlying asset hasn't moved much.

Long straddles can also be effective as a hedging tool during volatile periods. For example, if a trader has a large position in an underlying asset and wants to protect against potential losses without giving up the possibility of gains, a long straddle can provide this two-way protection. While this is generally a more expensive form of hedging compared to simply buying a protective put, it allows the trader to maintain full upside potential in highly uncertain market conditions. Implementing a long straddle in volatile markets involves several key steps, beginning with thorough market analysis. Start by identifying an underlying asset that you expect to experience a significant price move or increased volatility. This could be an individual stock, an ETF, or a market index. Consider both technical and fundamental factors that support your expectation of increased volatility or a large price move. Look for assets with upcoming events that could cause significant price swings, or those that have been showing signs of increasing volatility.

Once you've selected your underlying asset, choose an expiration date for your long straddle. In volatile markets, the choice of expiration is particularly crucial. If you're trading a straddle around a specific event, you'll typically want to choose an expiration date shortly after the event. For more general volatility plays, you might consider longer-term expirations to capture extended periods of market turbulence. Keep in mind that longer-term options will be more expensive but will give your thesis more time to play out. Selecting the appropriate strike price is crucial in constructing your long straddle, especially in volatile conditions. Typically, at-the-money options are used, meaning the strike price is as close as possible to the current price of the underlying asset. This provides a balanced exposure to moves in either direction. However, in highly volatile markets, some traders might choose to implement a slightly bullish or bearish bias by selecting a strike price slightly above or below the current asset price.

When you're ready to place the trade, enter the long straddle as a single order, specifying both the call and put legs simultaneously. This is particularly important in volatile markets where prices can change rapidly. Entering a single order ensures you get filled on both options at the same time, avoiding any risk of adverse price movements between separate orders. Most modern trading platforms allow you to enter straddle orders directly, simplifying the process. However, it's still important to double-check all the details before submitting your order to avoid any costly mistakes in fast-moving markets. Before entering the trade, it's crucial to set a clear exit strategy, which becomes even more critical in volatile conditions. Determine in advance at what profit level you'll close the position and at what loss level you'll exit to limit your downside. Many straddle traders aim to close the position if they achieve a certain percentage of profit, such as 50% or 100% of the initial investment. In volatile markets, you might consider using trailing stops to lock in profits as the underlying asset makes large moves. Similarly, having a predetermined stop-loss point can help limit losses if the underlying asset fails to make the anticipated move or if volatility decreases unexpectedly.

Once the trade is executed, it's important to monitor and manage the position actively, which is particularly crucial in volatile markets. Keep track of how the straddle's value changes in relation to movements in the underlying asset and changes in implied volatility. Be prepared to adjust or close the trade as market conditions change or as you approach expiration. In highly volatile conditions, some traders actively manage their straddles, potentially closing one side of the position if the underlying asset makes a significant move in one direction, leaving the other side open for potential further gains.

It's important to be aware of the risks associated with long straddles, especially in volatile markets. While the maximum loss is limited to the premium paid, this can still be a significant amount, particularly when option prices are inflated due to high implied volatility. Additionally, time decay works against long straddle positions, eroding their value as expiration approaches. This means that even if your volatility view is correct, you may still lose money if the anticipated price moves don't happen quickly enough or aren't large enough to overcome the impact of time decay. The long straddle offers traders a powerful tool to potentially profit from significant price movements and increased volatility without needing to predict the direction. It's particularly well-suited for volatile markets where large price swings are anticipated. However, it requires careful timing, active management, and a significant move in the underlying asset or spike in volatility to be profitable. Traders must weigh the potential for large profits against the high cost and the risk of losing the entire premium paid if the anticipated volatility doesn't materialize. When used appropriately, long straddles can be a valuable addition to a trader's strategic toolkit for navigating and potentially profiting from turbulent market conditions.

The Long Strangle

The long strangle is a popular options strategy that, like the long straddle, allows traders to profit from significant price movements in either direction without needing to predict whether the move will be up or down. However, the strangle differs from the straddle in its structure and risk-reward profile. This non-directional strategy involves simultaneously buying an out-of-the-money call option and an out-of-the-money put option with the same expiration date on the same underlying asset. The long strangle is particularly useful in volatile markets when a trader anticipates a large price move but is unsure of the direction and wants a less expensive alternative to the straddle. At its core, a long strangle consists of two options contracts: an out-of-the-money call and an out-of-the-money put. Both options have the same underlying asset and expiration date, but different strike prices. The trader buys both options, which means they're paying two premiums and taking on the role of the option holder for both contracts. This dual purchase gives the trader the right, but not the obligation, to both buy (via the call) and sell (via the put) the underlying asset at their respective strike prices before or at expiration. In volatile markets, this structure allows traders to potentially capitalize on large price swings while typically requiring a lower initial investment compared to a straddle.

The basic mechanics of a long strangle can be understood by examining its components. The long call option gives the trader the right to buy the underlying asset at the higher strike price. As the asset's price increases above this strike price plus the total premium paid, this option becomes profitable. Conversely, the long put option gives the trader the right to sell the underlying asset at the lower strike price. As the asset's price decreases below this strike price minus the total premium paid, this option becomes profitable. The combination of these two out-of-the-money options creates a position that can profit from a move in either direction, as long as the move is large enough to overcome the total cost of the premiums. This structure is particularly advantageous in volatile markets where large price swings are more likely to occur.

The profit potential for a long strangle is theoretically unlimited on the upside (due to the call option) and limited only by the underlying asset reaching zero on the downside (due to the put option). The maximum loss is limited to the total premium paid for both options, which occurs if the underlying asset's price at expiration is between the two strike prices, causing both options to expire worthless. The break-even points for a strangle are calculated by adding the total premium paid to the call strike price for the upside breakeven, and subtracting the total premium paid from the put strike price for the downside breakeven. In volatile markets, these break-even points may be reached more quickly or frequently due to larger price movements.

Long strangles are particularly useful in several scenarios common to volatile markets. One of the most frequent applications is when a trader anticipates a significant market-moving event but is uncertain about the direction of the move and wants a less expensive alternative to a straddle. This could be ahead of earnings announcements, major economic data releases, central bank decisions, or geopolitical events that could cause large price swings. By implementing a long strangle, the trader can potentially profit regardless of whether the news is positive or negative, as long as the resulting price move is large enough to surpass one of the break-even points. The wider break-even range of a strangle compared to a straddle means that while a larger move is needed for profitability, the strategy is less expensive to implement, which can be advantageous in volatile markets where option premiums are often inflated.

Another scenario where long strangles can be valuable in volatile markets is when a trader expects an increase in volatility itself. If a trader believes that market turbulence is about to increase significantly, a long strangle can provide exposure to this anticipated spike in volatility at a lower cost than a straddle. This makes strangles a popular choice for traders who have a view on volatility rather than on price direction and are willing to accept a larger required price move for profitability in exchange for lower upfront costs. In highly volatile markets, the potential for large price swings can make this trade-off particularly attractive. Long strangles can also be used as a hedging tool in volatile market conditions. For example, if a trader has a large position in an underlying asset and wants to protect against potential extreme losses without giving up too much upside potential, a long strangle can provide this two-way protection at a lower cost than a straddle. While this is still a more expensive form of hedging compared to simply buying a protective put, it allows the trader to maintain full upside potential beyond the call strike price. This can be particularly valuable in volatile markets where the potential for both significant losses and substantial gains is heightened.

Implementing a long strangle in volatile markets involves several key steps, beginning with thorough market analysis. Start by identifying an underlying asset that you expect to experience a significant price move or increased volatility. This could be an individual stock, an ETF, or a market index. Consider both technical and fundamental factors that support your expectation of increased volatility or a large price move. Look for assets with upcoming events that could cause significant price swings, or those that have been showing signs of increasing volatility. In turbulent market conditions, it's especially important to assess not just the potential for price movement, but also the current levels of implied volatility, as this will affect option prices and the overall cost of the strategy.

Once you've selected your underlying asset, choose an expiration date for your long strangle. In volatile markets, the choice of expiration is particularly crucial. If you're trading a strangle around a specific event, you'll typically want to choose an expiration date shortly after the event. For more general volatility plays, you might consider longer-term expirations to capture extended periods of market turbulence. Keep in mind that longer-term options will be more expensive but will give your thesis more time to play out. In highly volatile conditions, you might also consider using multiple expiration dates to create a time spread or calendar strangle, which can help manage the impact of time decay. Selecting the appropriate strike prices is crucial in constructing your long strangle, especially in volatile conditions. Unlike a straddle, which typically uses at-the-money options, a strangle uses out-of-the-money options. You'll need to choose a call strike price above the current asset price and a put strike price below it. The wider the spread between these strike prices, the less expensive the strangle will be to implement, but the larger the price move required for profitability. Your choice of strike prices should reflect your assessment of the potential magnitude of the price move and your risk tolerance. In volatile markets, you might consider using slightly closer strike prices than you would in calmer conditions, as the potential for large moves is increased.

When you're ready to place the trade, enter the long strangle as a single order, specifying both the call and put legs simultaneously. This is particularly important in volatile markets where prices can change rapidly. Entering a single order ensures you get filled on both options at the same time, avoiding any risk of adverse price movements between separate orders. Most modern trading platforms allow you to enter strangle orders directly, simplifying the process. However, it's still important to double-check all the details before submitting your order to avoid any costly mistakes in fast-moving markets. Consider using limit orders rather than market orders to ensure you don't overpay for the options, especially in volatile conditions where bid-ask spreads may be wider. Before entering the trade, it's crucial to set a clear exit strategy, which becomes even more critical in volatile conditions. Determine in advance at what profit level you'll close the position and at what loss level you'll exit to limit your downside. Many strangle traders aim to close the position if they achieve a certain percentage of profit, such as 50% or 100% of the initial investment. In volatile markets, you might consider using trailing stops to lock in profits as the underlying asset makes large moves. Similarly, having a predetermined stop-loss point can help limit losses if the underlying asset fails to make the anticipated move or if volatility decreases unexpectedly. It's also important to have a plan for managing the position if only one leg of the strangle becomes profitable.

Once the trade is executed, it's important to monitor and manage the position actively, which is particularly crucial in volatile markets. Keep track of how the strangle's value changes in relation to movements in the underlying asset and changes in implied volatility. Be prepared to adjust or close the trade as market conditions change or as you approach expiration. In highly volatile conditions, some traders actively manage their strangles, potentially closing one side of the position if the underlying asset makes a significant move in one direction, leaving the other side open for potential further gains. You might also consider rolling the position to a later expiration date if your volatility thesis remains intact but more time is needed for it to play out.

It's important to be aware of the risks associated with long strangles, especially in volatile markets. While the maximum loss is limited to the premium paid, the strategy requires a larger move in the underlying asset to be profitable compared to a straddle. Traders must weigh the lower cost and potential for large profits against the higher breakeven points and the risk of losing the entire premium paid if the anticipated move doesn't materialize. Additionally, time decay works against long strangle positions, eroding their value as expiration approaches. This means that even if your volatility view is correct, you may still lose money if the anticipated price moves don't happen quickly enough or aren't large enough to overcome the impact of time decay. The long strangle offers traders a way to potentially profit from significant price movements and increased volatility without needing to predict the direction, and at a lower cost than a straddle. This makes it a particularly attractive strategy for volatile markets where large price swings are anticipated but the direction is uncertain. By mastering this strategy, traders can expand their ability to navigate turbulent market conditions and capitalize on events that are expected to cause substantial price movements, while managing their risk through lower upfront costs. However, like all options strategies, success with long strangles in volatile markets requires thorough understanding, careful planning, and disciplined execution. When used appropriately, long strangles can be a valuable addition to a trader's strategic toolkit for potentially profiting from market turbulence while maintaining a defined risk profile.

The Short Straddle

The short straddle is an advanced options strategy that allows traders to potentially profit from a lack of significant price movement in the underlying asset, even in volatile market conditions. This neutral strategy involves simultaneously selling a call option and a put option with the same strike price and expiration date on the same underlying asset. The short straddle is designed to take advantage of time decay and potentially profit from overpriced options in high implied volatility environments, which are often characteristic of volatile markets. However, it's important to note that this strategy comes with unlimited risk potential and is generally considered suitable only for experienced options traders.

At its core, a short straddle consists of two options contracts: a short call and a short put. Both options have the same underlying asset, strike price, and expiration date. The trader sells both options, which means they're receiving two premiums and taking on the role of the option writer for both contracts. This dual sale obligates the trader to buy the underlying asset (if the put is exercised) or sell the underlying asset (if the call is exercised) at the strike price if the options are exercised by their respective holders.

The basic mechanics of a short straddle can be understood by examining its components. The short call option obligates the trader to sell the underlying asset at the strike price if the option is exercised. As the asset's price increases above the strike price plus the total premium received, this option position becomes unprofitable. Conversely, the short put option obligates the trader to buy the underlying asset at the strike price if the option is exercised. As the asset's price decreases below the strike price minus the total premium received, this option position becomes unprofitable. The combination of these two short options creates a position that can profit if the underlying asset remains close to the strike price, but can incur significant losses if the asset makes a large move in either direction.

The maximum profit for a short straddle is limited to the total premium received for both options, which occurs if the underlying asset's price at expiration is exactly at the strike price, causing both options to expire worthless. The potential loss, however, is theoretically unlimited on the upside (due to the short call) and limited only by the underlying asset reaching zero on the downside (due to the short put). The break-even points for a short straddle are calculated by adding and subtracting the total premium received from the strike price. Short straddles can be particularly useful in volatile markets under specific circumstances. One common application is when a trader expects the underlying asset to remain relatively stable in price, despite overall market volatility. This could occur when an asset has already made a significant move and the trader believes it will consolidate or when market volatility is high but concentrated in other sectors or assets. By implementing a short straddle, the trader can potentially profit from time decay and a potential decrease in implied volatility specific to that asset.

Another scenario where short straddles can be valuable in volatile markets is when implied volatility is unusually high for a particular asset. Options tend to be overpriced when implied volatility is elevated, which is often the case in volatile market conditions. Selling options in these conditions can be profitable if volatility subsequently decreases, even if the overall market remains turbulent. This makes short straddles a potential strategy for traders who believe that the market is overestimating the likelihood of a large price move for a specific asset. Short straddles can also be used as part of more complex options strategies or in conjunction with other positions to navigate volatile markets. For example, a trader might use a short straddle to generate income on a long stock position while simultaneously using other options to hedge against broad market volatility. This approach allows the trader to potentially benefit from asset-specific stability while protecting against wider market turbulence.

Implementing a short straddle in volatile markets involves several key steps, beginning with thorough market analysis. Start by identifying an underlying asset that you expect to remain stable in price, despite overall market volatility. This could be an individual stock, an ETF, or a market index. Consider both technical and fundamental factors that support your expectation of price stability for this particular asset. Look for assets trading in a tight range or showing signs of lower historical volatility compared to the broader market. Additionally, examine the implied volatility of the options on the asset, as higher implied volatility can lead to more attractive premium collection opportunities.

Once you've selected your underlying asset, choose an expiration date for your short straddle. In volatile markets, the choice of expiration is particularly crucial. Shorter-term expirations (30-45 days) are popular among many straddle sellers as they allow for more rapid time decay. However, in highly volatile conditions, longer-term expirations might be considered to provide more time for market turbulence to potentially subside. Consider your trading style, risk tolerance, and the characteristics of the underlying asset when making this decision. Selecting the appropriate strike price is crucial in constructing your short straddle, especially in volatile conditions. Typically, at-the-money options are used, meaning the strike price is as close as possible to the current price of the underlying asset. This provides the highest premium and the greatest profit potential if the asset remains stable. However, it also presents the highest risk if the asset price moves significantly, which is a real possibility in volatile markets. Some traders might consider using slightly out-of-the-money options to provide a small buffer against price movements, albeit at the cost of lower premium income.

When you're ready to place the trade, enter the short straddle as a single order, specifying both the call and put legs simultaneously. This is particularly important in volatile markets where prices can change rapidly. Entering a single order ensures you get filled on both options at the same time, avoiding any risk of adverse price movements between separate orders. Most modern trading platforms allow you to enter straddle orders directly, simplifying the process. However, it's still important to double-check all the details before submitting your order to avoid any costly mistakes in fast-moving markets. Before entering the trade, it's crucial to set a clear exit strategy, which becomes even more critical in volatile conditions. Determine in advance at what profit level you'll close the position and at what loss level you'll exit to limit your downside. Many short straddle traders aim to close the position when they've captured a certain percentage of the maximum potential profit, such as 50% or 75%. Setting a maximum acceptable loss is particularly important for short straddles due to the unlimited risk potential, especially in volatile markets where large, sudden price moves are more likely.

Once the trade is executed, it's critical to monitor and manage the position actively, which is particularly crucial in volatile markets. Keep track of how the straddle's value changes in relation to movements in the underlying asset and changes in implied volatility. Be prepared to adjust or close the trade as market conditions change or as you approach expiration. Some traders actively manage their short straddles, potentially rolling the position to a later expiration date or adjusting strike prices if the underlying asset moves away from the initial strike price. In highly volatile conditions, having a plan for quickly hedging or closing the position if it moves against you is essential.

It's extremely important to be aware of the risks associated with short straddles, particularly in volatile markets. The potential for unlimited losses means that risk management is crucial. Many traders use stop-loss orders or options to hedge their position. For example, a trader might buy out-of-the-money options to cap their potential losses, effectively turning the short straddle into an iron butterfly. Additionally, be aware of the risk of early assignment, especially if the underlying asset pays dividends or if one side of the straddle becomes deeply in-the-money, which is more likely in volatile conditions. Changes in implied volatility can significantly affect the value of a short straddle. Generally, a decrease in implied volatility will benefit the position, while an increase will hurt it. This sensitivity to volatility changes means that a straddle's value can fluctuate even if the underlying asset's price remains unchanged. In volatile markets, these fluctuations can be more pronounced, requiring closer monitoring and potentially more frequent adjustments.

In conclusion, the short straddle offers traders a way to potentially profit from price stability and time decay, even in volatile market conditions. However, it comes with significant risks that are amplified in turbulent markets. It's best suited for experienced options traders who have a thorough understanding of options mechanics, strong risk management skills, and the ability to monitor and adjust positions actively. When used appropriately and with proper risk controls, short straddles can be a valuable tool for generating income in specific situations within volatile markets. However, they should be approached with extreme caution and a full appreciation of their risk profile, particularly when overall market volatility is high.

The Short Strangle

The short strangle is an advanced options strategy that allows traders to potentially profit from a range-bound market, even in overall volatile conditions. This neutral strategy involves simultaneously selling an out-of-the-money call option and an out-of-the-money put option with the same expiration date on the same underlying asset. The short strangle is designed to take advantage of time decay and potentially profit from overpriced options in high implied volatility environments, which are often characteristic of volatile markets. However, like the short straddle, this strategy comes with significant risk and is generally considered suitable only for experienced options traders. At its core, a short strangle consists of two options contracts: a short call and a short put. Both options have the same underlying asset and expiration date, but different strike prices. The trader sells both options, which means they're receiving two premiums and taking on the role of the option writer for both contracts. This dual sale obligates the trader to buy the underlying asset (if the put is exercised) or sell the underlying asset (if the call is exercised) at their respective strike prices if the options are exercised by their holders.

The basic mechanics of a short strangle can be understood by examining its components. The short call option obligates the trader to sell the underlying asset at the higher strike price if the option is exercised. As the asset's price increases above this strike price plus the total premium received, this option position becomes unprofitable. Conversely, the short put option obligates the trader to buy the underlying asset at the lower strike price if the option is exercised. As the asset's price decreases below this strike price minus the total premium received, this option position becomes unprofitable. The combination of these two short out-of-the-money options creates a position that can profit if the underlying asset remains between the two strike prices, but can incur significant losses if the asset makes a large move beyond either strike price. The maximum profit for a short strangle is limited to the total premium received for both options, which occurs if the underlying asset's price at expiration is between the two strike prices, causing both options to expire worthless. The potential loss, however, is theoretically unlimited on the upside (due to the short call) and limited only by the underlying asset reaching zero on the downside (due to the short put). The break-even points for a short strangle are calculated by adding the total premium received to the call strike price for the upside breakeven, and subtracting the total premium received from the put strike price for the downside breakeven.

Short strangles can be particularly useful in volatile markets under specific circumstances. One common application is when a trader expects the underlying asset to remain within a specific price range, despite overall market volatility. This could occur when an asset has been trading in a defined channel or when technical analysis suggests strong support and resistance levels. By implementing a short strangle, the trader can potentially profit from time decay and a potential decrease in implied volatility specific to that asset, while allowing for some price movement within the chosen range.

Another scenario where short strangles can be valuable in volatile markets is when implied volatility is unusually high for a particular asset, but the trader believes that the actual price movement will be less extreme than what the options market is pricing in. Options tend to be overpriced when implied volatility is elevated, which is often the case in volatile market conditions. Selling options in these conditions can be profitable if volatility subsequently decreases or if the price movements are less significant than anticipated, even if the overall market remains turbulent. Short strangles can also be used as part of more complex options strategies or in conjunction with other positions to navigate volatile markets. For example, a trader might use a short strangle to generate income on a long stock position while simultaneously using other options or instruments to hedge against broad market volatility. This approach allows the trader to potentially benefit from asset-specific stability within a range while protecting against wider market turbulence.

Implementing a short strangle in volatile markets involves several key steps, beginning with thorough market analysis. Start by identifying an underlying asset that you expect to trade within a specific price range, despite overall market volatility. This could be an individual stock, an ETF, or a market index. Consider both technical and fundamental factors that support your expectation of range-bound trading for this particular asset. Look for assets with clear support and resistance levels or those showing signs of mean reversion tendencies. Additionally, examine the implied volatility of the options on the asset, as higher implied volatility can lead to more attractive premium collection opportunities. Once you've selected your underlying asset, choose an expiration date for your short strangle. In volatile markets, the choice of expiration is particularly crucial. Shorter-term expirations (30-45 days) are popular among many strangle sellers as they allow for more rapid time decay.

However, in highly volatile conditions, longer-term expirations might be considered to provide more time for market turbulence to potentially subside. Consider your trading style, risk tolerance, and the characteristics of the underlying asset when making this decision.

Selecting the appropriate strike prices is crucial in constructing your short strangle, especially in volatile conditions. Choose strike prices that are out-of-the-money and reflect the range in which you expect the underlying asset to trade. The width between the strike prices will determine your potential profit zone and the level of premium you can collect. Wider spreads between strike prices offer a larger potential profit zone but result in lower premium income. Narrower spreads increase premium income but provide a smaller range for profitable price movement. In volatile markets, you might consider using wider spreads to account for potentially larger price swings.

When you're ready to place the trade, enter the short strangle as a single order, specifying both the call and put legs simultaneously. This is particularly important in volatile markets where prices can change rapidly. Entering a single order ensures you get filled on both options at the same time, avoiding any risk of adverse price movements between separate orders. Most modern trading platforms allow you to enter strangle orders directly, simplifying the process. However, it's still important to double-check all the details before submitting your order to avoid any costly mistakes in fast-moving markets. Before entering the trade, it's crucial to set a clear exit strategy, which becomes even more critical in volatile conditions. Determine in advance at what profit level you'll close the position and at what loss level you'll exit to limit your downside. Many short strangle traders aim to close the position when they've captured a certain percentage of the maximum potential profit, such as 50% or 75%. Setting a maximum acceptable loss is particularly important for short strangles due to the unlimited risk potential, especially in volatile markets where large, sudden price moves are more likely.

Once the trade is executed, it's critical to monitor and manage the position actively, which is particularly crucial in volatile markets. Keep track of how the strangle's value changes in relation to movements in the underlying asset and changes in implied volatility. Be prepared to adjust or close the trade as market conditions change or as you approach expiration. Some traders actively manage their short strangles, potentially rolling the position to a later expiration date or adjusting strike prices if the underlying asset moves towards or beyond one of the strike prices. In highly volatile conditions, having a plan for quickly hedging or closing the position if it moves against you is essential. It's extremely important to be aware of the risks associated with short strangles, particularly in volatile markets. The potential for significant or unlimited losses means that risk management is crucial. Many traders use stop-loss orders or options to hedge their position. For example, a trader might buy further out-of-the-money options to cap their potential losses, effectively turning the short strangle into an iron condor.

Additionally, be aware of the risk of early assignment, especially if the underlying asset pays dividends or if one side of the strangle becomes in-the-money, which is more likely in volatile conditions.

Changes in implied volatility can significantly affect the value of a short strangle. Generally, a decrease in implied volatility will benefit the position, while an increase will hurt it. This sensitivity to volatility changes means that a strangle's value can fluctuate even if the underlying asset's price remains within the desired range. In volatile markets, these fluctuations can be more pronounced, requiring closer monitoring and potentially more frequent adjustments. The short strangle offers traders a way to potentially profit from range-bound price action and time decay, even in volatile market conditions. However, it comes with significant risks that are amplified in turbulent markets. It's best suited for experienced options traders who have a thorough understanding of options mechanics, strong risk management skills, and the ability to monitor and adjust positions actively. When used appropriately and with proper risk controls, short strangles can be a valuable tool for generating income in specific situations within volatile markets. However, they should be approached with extreme caution and a full appreciation of their risk profile, particularly when overall market volatility is high.

The Volatility Index (VIX) Options

The Volatility Index (VIX), often referred to as the "fear gauge" of the market, is a popular measure of the stock market's expectation of volatility over the next 30 days. VIX options are derivative contracts based on the VIX index, allowing traders to directly speculate on or hedge against changes in market volatility. These unique instruments have become increasingly popular among sophisticated traders and investors, especially during periods of market turbulence.

At their core, VIX options are similar to standard equity options in structure, offering both call and put contracts with various strike prices and expiration dates. However, the underlying asset – the VIX index itself – behaves quite differently from stocks or other traditional assets. The VIX is not a tangible asset that can be bought or sold directly, but rather a mathematical construct based on the implied volatilities of S&P 500 index options. The basic mechanics of VIX options can be understood by examining their relation to the VIX index. A call option on the VIX gives the holder the right to "buy" the VIX at a specific strike price, profiting if the index rises above that level. Conversely, a put option on the VIX gives the holder the right to "sell" the VIX at a specific strike price, profiting if the index falls below that level. However, since the VIX itself cannot be bought or sold, these options are cash-settled, meaning that at expiration, the holder receives the difference in cash between the strike price and the VIX level (for in-the-money options).

VIX options are particularly useful in several scenarios, especially in volatile market conditions. One common application is as a hedging tool against market downturns. Since the VIX tends to spike when the stock market experiences sharp declines, buying VIX calls can provide a form of portfolio insurance. If the market drops and volatility increases, the value of the VIX calls is likely to rise, potentially offsetting losses in other parts of the portfolio.

Another scenario where VIX options can be valuable is when a trader wants to directly speculate on future volatility levels. If a trader believes that market volatility is likely to increase – perhaps due to anticipated economic data releases, geopolitical events, or other factors – they might buy VIX calls. Conversely, if they expect volatility to decrease, they might buy VIX puts or sell VIX calls.

VIX options can also be used in combination with other options strategies to create more complex volatility trades. For example, a trader might simultaneously buy VIX calls and sell equity index puts to create a position that profits from an increase in implied volatility relative to realized volatility. Implementing a VIX options strategy involves several key steps, beginning with a thorough analysis of current market conditions and future expectations. Start by assessing the current level of the VIX index relative to its historical range. Consider factors that could impact future volatility, such as upcoming economic reports, central bank meetings, political events, or seasonal patterns in market volatility. Once you've formed a view on future volatility, choose the appropriate VIX option strategy. If you expect volatility to increase, you might consider buying VIX calls or call spreads. If you anticipate a decrease in volatility, VIX puts or put spreads might be appropriate. For more neutral views, strategies like straddles or strangles on the VIX could be considered.

Selecting the right expiration date is crucial when trading VIX options. The VIX is a mean-reverting index, meaning it tends to return to its long-term average over time. Therefore, longer-dated options allow more time for your volatility thesis to play out but are also more expensive. Shorter-dated options are cheaper but require more precise timing. Consider the timeframe of your volatility expectations when choosing an expiration date. Choosing the appropriate strike price is another important consideration. At-the-money options provide the most direct exposure to changes in the VIX but are also the most expensive. Out-of-the-money options are cheaper and can provide leveraged exposure if your view is correct, but they also have a higher probability of expiring worthless. Your choice of strike price should reflect both your market outlook and your risk tolerance.

When you're ready to execute the trade, enter your VIX option order carefully. Due to the specialized nature of these products, liquidity can sometimes be an issue, especially for further out-of-the-money or longer-dated options. Use limit orders rather than market orders to ensure you don't overpay, and be patient in getting your order filled at a reasonable price. Before entering the trade, set clear profit targets and stop-loss levels. VIX options can be quite volatile themselves, and having predetermined exit points can help manage risk and emotions during turbulent market periods. Consider using option spreads to define your maximum potential loss if you're uncomfortable with the unlimited risk of naked long options. Once the trade is executed, monitor it closely. VIX options can move quickly in response to changes in market sentiment or actual volatility events. Be prepared to adjust your position if market conditions change significantly or if your original thesis proves incorrect.

It's important to be aware of the unique risks associated with VIX options. The VIX index itself is not directly tradable, which can lead to discrepancies between the behavior of VIX options and the underlying index. Additionally, VIX options are European-style and can only be exercised at expiration, which can impact their behavior, especially near expiry. The volatility of volatility (often referred to as "vol of vol") is another crucial factor to consider. VIX options can experience rapid and significant price swings, even more so than options on individual stocks or equity indices. This heightened sensitivity to market movements means that risk management is paramount when trading VIX options.

Another unique aspect of VIX options is their settlement process. VIX options settle to the Special Opening Quotation (SOQ) of the VIX on the expiration date, which is calculated using the opening prices of S&P 500 options. This settlement process can sometimes lead to surprises, as the SOQ can differ significantly from the previous day's closing VIX level. VIX options offer traders and investors a powerful tool for directly trading volatility expectations or hedging against market turbulence. They provide unique exposure to market sentiment and can be valuable components of sophisticated trading and risk management strategies. However, due to their complex nature and the specialized knowledge required to trade them effectively, VIX options are best suited for experienced traders who thoroughly understand both options mechanics and the behavior of volatility in financial markets. When used appropriately, VIX options can be a valuable addition to a trader's toolkit, especially in navigating and potentially profiting from volatile market conditions.

Conclusion

"The secret of getting ahead is getting started."
– Mark Twain

As we reach the end of our comprehensive journey through the world of options trading, it's important to take a moment to reflect on the key concepts and strategies we've explored. This book has covered a wide range of topics, from the fundamentals of options to advanced strategies for various market conditions. Let's recap some of the most crucial points and consider how they fit into your overall approach to options trading. We began our exploration with the basics of options, understanding that these financial derivatives provide the right, but not the obligation, to buy or sell an underlying asset at a predetermined price within a specific time frame. This fundamental characteristic is what gives options their unique flexibility and power in the world of financial instruments.

We delved into the two primary types of options - calls and puts - and how they can be used to express bullish or bearish views on an underlying asset. Call options, giving the holder the right to buy, are typically used in bullish scenarios, while put options, conferring the right to sell, are often employed in bearish situations. However, as we discovered throughout the book, the versatility of options allows for much more nuanced strategies than simple directional bets. The concept of option "moneyness" - whether an option is in-the-money, at-the-money, or out-of-the-money - was introduced as a crucial factor in understanding option behavior and pricing. We learned how this status affects an option's intrinsic and time value, and how it influences the choice of options in various strategies.

Time decay, or theta, emerged as a critical concept in options trading. We explored how the passage of time affects option prices and how different strategies can be employed to either benefit from or mitigate the effects of time decay. This led us to understand the importance of choosing appropriate expiration dates for our options trades, balancing the need for time for our thesis to play out against the erosive effects of theta. Implied volatility was another key concept we tackled. We learned how this forward-looking measure of market expectations can significantly impact option prices and how traders can potentially profit from changes in implied volatility, not just directional moves in the underlying asset. This understanding opened up a whole new dimension of options trading, beyond simple price speculation.

As we moved into more advanced territory, we explored a variety of options strategies designed for different market outlooks and risk tolerances. Let's briefly recap some of the key strategies we covered:

1) Covered Calls: This strategy, involving holding a long stock position and selling call options against it, was presented as a way to generate additional income from

a portfolio and potentially provide some downside protection. We discussed how it can be particularly effective in sideways or slightly bullish markets.

2) Protective Puts: We explored how buying put options can act as a form of insurance for long stock positions, protecting against potential downside while still allowing for upside participation. This strategy highlighted the power of options as risk management tools.

3) Bull Call Spreads and Bear Put Spreads: These vertical spread strategies were introduced as ways to implement directional views with defined risk and potentially lower cost compared to outright long options positions. We discussed how they can be effective in moderately bullish or bearish markets, respectively.

4) Iron Condors: This neutral strategy, combining a bull put spread and a bear call spread, was presented as a way to potentially profit from range-bound markets. We explored how it can be used to generate income in low volatility environments.

5) Straddles and Strangles: These strategies, involving buying both call and put options, were discussed as ways to potentially profit from significant price movements without needing to predict direction. We examined how they can be particularly useful ahead of events that might cause large price swings.

6) Calendar Spreads: This time-based strategy, involving selling short-term options and buying longer-term options, was explored as a way to potentially profit from time decay while maintaining exposure to potential future price movements.

7) Ratio Spreads: We delved into these more advanced strategies that involve buying and selling options in unequal quantities, discussing how they can be used to create customized risk-reward profiles.

8) Synthetic Positions: We explored how options can be used to create positions that mimic stock ownership or short selling, often with lower capital requirements or reduced risk.

Throughout our discussion of these strategies, we consistently emphasized the importance of understanding the risk-reward profiles, potential outcomes, and specific market conditions for which each strategy is best suited. We stressed that no single strategy is universally superior, and that the choice of strategy should always be guided by your market outlook, risk tolerance, and overall investment goals. In our exploration of volatility-focused strategies, we introduced the concept of trading volatility itself, rather than just directional price movements. We discussed the VIX index and VIX options as tools for directly speculating on or hedging against changes in market volatility. This advanced topic highlighted the multidimensional nature of options trading and the sophisticated strategies available to experienced traders.

Throughout the book, we consistently emphasized the critical importance of risk management. We discussed various techniques for managing risk, including position sizing, setting stop-loss orders, and using option spreads to define maximum potential losses. The concept of risk-reward ratio was a recurring theme, underlining the importance of ensuring that potential profits justify the risks taken in any options trade. As we conclude this book, it's crucial to understand that what we've covered here, while comprehensive, is just the beginning of your options trading journey. The world of options is vast and complex, and even experienced traders continue to learn and refine their skills throughout their careers. Continuous learning is not just beneficial in options trading; it's absolutely essential. Markets are dynamic, constantly evolving entities. New products are introduced, regulations change, and market dynamics shift over time. Staying informed about these changes and continuously updating your knowledge is crucial for long-term success in options trading.

Moreover, the strategies we've discussed in this book are not meant to be rigid formulas, but rather frameworks that you can adapt and modify based on your own experiences and market observations. As you gain more experience, you'll likely develop your own variations on these strategies or even create entirely new approaches tailored to your specific trading style and goals. Practice is equally important. Options trading is not just about understanding concepts; it's about applying them effectively in real-world market conditions. Paper trading, or simulated trading with virtual money, is an excellent way to gain experience without risking real capital. Many brokers offer paper trading platforms that allow you to test strategies and get a feel for how options behave in various market conditions. Even after you begin trading with real money, it's advisable to start small and gradually increase your position sizes as you gain confidence and experience. Remember, even the most successful options traders had to start somewhere, and they likely made their fair share of mistakes along the way. The key is to learn from these mistakes and continuously improve your trading process.

Keeping a detailed trading journal can be an invaluable tool in this learning process. Record not just your trades, but also your reasoning behind each trade, your expectations, and the actual outcomes. Regularly reviewing this journal can help you identify patterns in your trading, both successful and unsuccessful, and refine your approach over time. Stay curious and open-minded. The options market is constantly evolving, and new strategies or variations on existing strategies are always being developed. Attend webinars, read books and articles, and consider joining options trading communities or forums where you can exchange ideas with other traders. However, always approach new ideas with a critical mind and thoroughly understand any strategy before implementing it with real money. One of the most crucial steps in becoming a successful options trader is developing a comprehensive, personalized trading plan. This plan should serve as your roadmap, guiding your trading decisions and helping you maintain discipline in the face of market volatility and emotional pressures.

Your trading plan should begin with a clear statement of your overall financial goals. Are you trading options to generate additional income, to grow your wealth over the long term, or to hedge other investments? Your goals will inform every other aspect of your plan, from the strategies you employ to the level of risk you're willing to take. Next, consider your risk tolerance. Options trading can involve significant risk, and it's crucial to be honest with yourself about how much risk you're comfortable taking. Your risk tolerance will influence the types of strategies you use, the size of your positions, and how you manage your overall portfolio. Your plan should also include specific criteria for entering and exiting trades. What technical or fundamental factors will you look for before entering a trade? At what profit level will you close out winning positions? How will you manage losing trades? Having these criteria defined in advance can help remove emotion from your trading decisions and promote consistency in your approach.

Time management is another important aspect of your trading plan. How much time can you realistically devote to researching, executing, and managing your trades? Some options strategies require more active management than others, so choose strategies that align with the time you have available. Include a section on continuous education and improvement in your plan. Set goals for expanding your knowledge, whether it's learning a new strategy each month, attending a certain number of trading webinars per year, or regularly reviewing and analyzing your past trades. Risk management should be a central component of your trading plan. Define how much of your total trading capital you're willing to risk on any single trade, and how you'll allocate your capital across different strategies or underlying assets. Consider incorporating rules for portfolio diversification to manage overall risk. Your plan should also address how you'll handle the psychological aspects of trading. Options trading can be emotionally challenging, with the potential for both significant gains and losses. Define strategies for maintaining discipline, managing stress, and avoiding common psychological pitfalls like overtrading or revenge trading.

Once you've developed your trading plan, the next crucial step is to stick to it. This can be more challenging than it sounds, especially when faced with the day-to-day volatility of the markets. It's easy to be swayed by emotions, whether it's the fear of missing out on a seemingly great opportunity or the panic that can set in during market downturns. Remember, your trading plan was developed thoughtfully, taking into account your goals, risk tolerance, and overall strategy. It's designed to guide you through various market conditions, not just when things are going well. Deviating from your plan on a whim can expose you to risks you're not prepared for and can lead to inconsistent results.

That said, sticking to your plan doesn't mean never making changes. As you gain experience and as market conditions evolve, you may find that certain aspects of your plan need to be adjusted. The key is to make these adjustments thoughtfully and systematically, not in the heat of the moment during trading hours. Regularly review and evaluate your trading plan. Set aside time each month or quarter to assess how well your plan is working. Are you meeting your goals? Are your risk management strategies effective? Are there new strategies or market developments you need to incorporate? This regular review process allows you to refine and improve your plan over time, ensuring it remains relevant and effective.

Options trading offers a world of opportunities for those willing to invest the time and effort to truly understand it. The strategies and concepts we've explored in this book provide a solid foundation, but they are just the beginning. Success in options trading comes from continuous learning, diligent practice, and the development and disciplined execution of a personalized trading plan. Remember that every successful trader has faced challenges and setbacks along the way. What sets them apart is their commitment to learning from these experiences and continuously improving their craft. Approach your options trading journey with patience, persistence, and a willingness to learn, and you'll be well-positioned to navigate the complex but potentially rewarding world of options trading.

As you move forward, stay informed about market developments, remain flexible in your thinking, and always prioritize risk management. With dedication and the right approach, options trading can become a powerful tool in your overall investment strategy, offering opportunities for income generation, capital growth, and portfolio protection. Thank you for joining me on this exploration of options trading. I wish you the best of luck in your trading endeavors and encourage you to approach the markets with confidence, caution, and an endless curiosity to learn and grow as a trader. The journey of mastering options trading is ongoing, but with the foundation you've gained from this book and a commitment to continuous improvement, you're well-equipped to take on the challenges and opportunities that lie ahead. Happy trading!